TWENTIETH CENTURY VIEWS

The aim of this series is to present the best in contemporary critical opinion on major authors, providing a twentieth century perspective on their changing status in an era of profound revaluation.

PINTER

A COLLECTION OF CRITICAL ESSAYS

Edited by
Arthur Ganz

Prentice-Hall, Inc. 

Englewood Cliffs, N.J.

Library of Congress Cataloging in Publication Data

GANZ, ARTHUR F comp.
Pinter, a collection of critical essays.

(A Spectrum Book: Twentieth century views)
Bibliography: p.
1. Pinter, Harold, 1930–
PR6066.I53Z647 822'.9'14 72-8031
ISBN 0-13-676387-1
ISBN 0-13-676379-0 (pbk)

Quotations from the following plays of Harold Pinter are used by permission of Grove Press, Inc., and Methuen & Co. Limited.

The Birthday Party. © 1959 by Harold Pinter.
The Caretaker. © 1960 by Theatre Promotions Ltd.
Collection. © 1962 by Harold Pinter.
The Dumb Waiter. © 1960 by Harold Pinter.
The Dwarfs. © 1961 by Harold Pinter, Ltd.
The Homecoming. © 1965 and 1966 by Harold Pinter, Ltd.
Landscape. © 1968 by Harold Pinter, Ltd.
Old Times. © 1971 by Harold Pinter, Ltd.
A Night Out. © 1961 by Harold Pinter, Ltd.
Night School. © 1967 by Harold Pinter, Ltd.
The Room. © 1960 by Harold Pinter.
Silence. © 1969 by Harold Pinter, Ltd.
A Slight Ache. © 1961 by Harold Pinter, Ltd.

10 9 8 7 6 5 4 3 2

PRENTICE-HALL INTERNATIONAL, INC. (*London*)
PRENTICE-HALL OF AUSTRALIA, PTY. LTD. (*Sydney*)
PRENTICE-HALL OF CANADA, LTD. (*Toronto*)
PRENTICE-HALL OF INDIA PRIVATE LIMITED (*New Delhi*)
PRENTICE-HALL OF JAPAN, INC. (*Tokyo*)

Contents

PINTER

Introduction

by Arthur Ganz

I.

Although Harold Pinter once said that his plays were about "the weasel under the cocktail cabinet," a recent interviewer claims that Pinter considers this remark meaningless and made it only "to frustrate this line of inquiry." [1] That it was intended to be cryptic is entirely possible, but that it is meaningless is doubtful; for, whatever Pinter's intentions, this metaphor suggests much that is central to his work. (Indeed, if the conjunction of Harold Pinter and Oscar Wilde were not so improbable, one might suppose that Pinter, idly perusing *Lady Windermere's Fan,* had been struck by Lord Darlington's comment when asked to elucidate one of his witticisms: "I think I had better not, Duchess. Now-a-days to be intelligible is to be found out.") Pinter shares the reluctance of many writers to have the full evocative experience of the work of art reduced, or altered, to an intellectual formulation. But for playgoers and readers sufficiently moved or intrigued to search for understanding, this remark is as near as Pinter himself has come to answering the nagging questions invariably aroused by a first acquaintance with his plays: who are these people? where do they come from? why do they behave in such extraordinary ways? what, in fact, are these plays all about? That they are about something significant is suggested by the insistent nature of the questions. If it were merely that odd pieces of the exposition had been left out, one might be curious, perhaps even a little annoyed at the writer for being careless or pointlessly tantalizing. But these are not the reactions that the plays evoke. They have

[1] The phrase is quoted in John Russell Taylor, *Anger and After* (Harmondsworth: Penguin Books, 1966), p. 285. The denial is referred to in Mel Gussow, "A Conversation [Pause] with Harold Pinter," *The New York Times Magazine,* December 5, 1971, p. 42.

the power to draw us into their world and to make us believe that, when we have found the answers to the questions that disturb us, we will not merely have acquired information about a rather curious group of people; we will have found out something crucial about ourselves. Behind the unhappy letters to the newspapers demanding more facts, which productions of a Pinter play tend to induce, or behind the essay complaining that the mystery is mere theatrical trickery, one senses that someone has been aroused to anxiety by glimpsing in one of those Pinter rooms a significant symbol of human life.

Through the ability to project such symbols onto the stage in powerful and intriguing terms Pinter has become, in hardly more than a decade, the most admired playwright to appear in the English-speaking theatre since Samuel Beckett.[2] The elusive yet hauntingly suggestive nature of these symbols has made him almost as widely discussed, for Pinter seems paradoxically to demand analysis even as he frustrates inquiry. His comment about the weasel and the cocktail cabinet is a case in point. The arresting metaphor (Pinter wrote a great deal of poetry before turning to playwriting in his late twenties) denies us direct information but insists that we look intently at what it evokes symbolically. If the cocktail cabinet calls up the vulgar rituals, the would-be elegances of modern middle-class life, then the weasel lurking astonishingly beneath that piece of furniture suggests the violence and bestiality that lies beneath the surface of our society and our selves. Beyond question, Pinter's metaphor does delineate much of what the plays are about. From the vicious attack that explodes at the climax of his first play, *The Room,* to the subtle struggle for psychological power that dominates his latest, *Old Times,* Pinter's plays have dealt with the malignant element usually hidden in human life.

But Pinter's comment, however illuminating, does no more than imply the nature and range (comparatively narrow) of his subject matter. It does not delineate that subject in any detail, nor does it suggest the special qualities of Pinter's style, which is so much a part of his meaning. For with Pinter—who works so much in terms

[2] Because Beckett is his own translator, the English versions of his plays must be considered as much originals as the French. Pinter is a professed admirer of Beckett, whose influence he acknowledges. See Martin Esslin, "Godot and His Children: the Theatre of Samuel Beckett and Harold Pinter," *Experimental Drama,* 14 (1965), 128–46.

of images and symbols—the manner of expression is a necessary way of conveying what is expressed. The most distinctive elements in Pinter's dramatic technique are the ambiguity that surrounds events, the mysterious behavior of characters, the near omnipresence of menace, and the silences and other special verbal characteristics. It is worth seeing how each of these elements carries part of Pinter's meaning before trying to establish our sense of the play as a whole.

II.

The most immediately discernible of these elements is undoubtedly the difficulty in verifying events. The plays are full of unanswered questions. Who is Riley in *The Room*? What organization has Stanley betrayed in *The Birthday Party*? What is Davies' real name in *The Caretaker*? Has Stella really committed adultery in *The Collection*? Pinter, an experienced theatre worker, must have known that any benefits gained by creating suspense and rousing the audience's curiosity would probably be outweighed by the likelihood of producing confusion and hostility. Indeed, at an early London production two of his plays (*The Room* and *The Dumb Waiter* at the Royal Court in March of 1960), Pinter placed in the program a note defending their obscurity. It is worth quoting in part, both for what it says and for what it does not say:

> The desire for verification is understandable but cannot always be satisfied. There are no hard distinctions between what is real and what is unreal, nor between what is true and what is false. The thing is not necessarily either true or false: it can be both true and false. The assumption that to verify what has happened and what is happening presents few problems I take to be inaccurate. A character on the stage who can present no convincing argument or information as to his past experience, his present behaviour or his aspirations, nor give a comprehensive analysis of his motives is as legitimate and as worthy of attention as one who, alarmingly, can do all these things. The more acute the experience, the less articulate its expression.[3]

This serious, defensive, even belligerent statement seems at first glance to offer a metaphysical vision of the unity of opposites. But

[3] Quoted in Martin Esslin, *The Peopled Wound: The Work of Harold Pinter* (New York: Doubleday Anchor Books, 1970), pp. 33–34.

when Pinter says that there are "no hard distinctions between what is real and what is unreal" and that a thing "can be both true and false," he is saying something much simpler and more familiar, that facts and impressions come to us filtered through the unreliable senses of unreliable people and that what is true for one person is false for another. The notion, however, that one man's meat is another man's poison was not new when Pirandello made a part of his drama out of it, and it has not become so since. What is novel, powerful, and daring is Pinter's ability to make passages of dialogue into moments that suddenly and powerfully illuminate this idea and give it theatrical life. Moreover, the removal of our certainty about the common events of external reality always serves in his work to focus our attention on the greater truths of the inner reality. By making unverifiable, and thus in effect removing, the surface layer of fact that covers our lives, he exposes the terrible facts beneath, which the experience of ordinary life makes all too easily verifiable.

In *The Room,* for example, the landlord, Mr. Kidd, says that he does not know, or at any rate no longer counts, the number of floors in his house. A moment later he announces that he thinks his mother was Jewish. "I think my mum was a Jewess. Yes, I wouldn't be surprised to learn that she was a Jewess." Pinter knows very well that only the most absent-minded of householders is in ignorance of the number of floors in his establishment or of his mother's religious background; but he also knows—and has the literary power to make us recognize or reaffirm—that most of us, like Mr. Kidd, are not quite sure of the dimensions of the part of the world which we inhabit, of how far our responsibility and our authority extend, and he also knows that many of us, whatever our mothers' ostensible backgrounds, feel our separateness as something congenital, sense ourselves as descended from an alien breed.

It is true, then, that many facts in a Pinter play are not given to us (facts that are often literally verifiable, Pinter's youthful protestations to the contrary), but it is also true that the significant things we need to know are never left out and that these are brought into sharp symbolic focus by the blurring of detail. To take one further example, probably the most blatant denial of information in Pinter's work comes in *The Collection.* We never know why Stella has told her husband, James, that she has betrayed him. Nor are we even sure that she has done so, for though Bill, the man in question, confesses under dramatically convincing duress that they did nothing but talk about the possibility of sexual relations, at the end of the play Pinter once again raises the question of the reality of the affair. What we do know beyond question is that each character has been tormented by the possibility of the relationship, that each character has used the occasion to torment others, to threaten, to rouse jealousy, to exert power. With perfect clarity Pinter has portrayed in both the homosexual and the heterosexual households the lurking presence of pride, fear, hostility, of love turning to boredom or to imprisonment. The human cruelty that *The Collection* reveals has assuredly been revealed before; it is great and traditional material, Strindbergian in its fierce intensity (in London *The Collection* was performed on a double bill with a play of Strindberg's); yet it is characteristically Pinter in its elusive, subtle, and elegant style.

What is true of Pinter's handling of event is also true of his handling of character. (Event and character are obviously so interlocked that a division between them tends always to be arbitrary; the distinction is worth drawing here for the light it sheds on the plays.) When he tells us, in the program note quoted above, that a character who cannot describe his past, present, or future or "give a comprehensive analysis of his motives is as legitimate and as worthy of attention as one who, alarmingly, can do all these things," he is not professing a special interest in amnesiacs. Nor is he merely suggesting that to be lost in time, to be unsure of the significance of one's personal history, to lack "identity" is inherent in the human condition as we know it in our world, though that is indeed part of what he means. Beyond this consideration Pinter wishes to shift emphasis away from the psychological investigation of character. Rare as the person is, either in literature or in life, who can on short notice "give a comprehensive analysis of his motives," authors prepared to do so on behalf of their characters have been comparatively common in modern drama. A figure such as Hedda Gabler is a richly developed psychological entity, to a considerable degree subject to analysis as people in life are. Many characters in the older drama, however, including many whom we sense as supremely "real," are not amenable to such investigation. Even so great and vivid a figure as Falstaff lives through the power of language rather than through our knowledge of his childhood or his inner life.

Pinter, then, like other writers in recent years, treats character in something nearer the classic mode. Though the notable personages of his plays—Goldberg, Davies, Max, for example—have the life and immediacy of all great dramatic characterizations, their vitality depends on the richness of their special language and on Pinter's ability to make them symbolically suggestive. The heart of their mystery is not to be plucked out with the tools of psychology.

The danger for a writer who does not insist on psychology in his treatment of character is that he will become a puppet master, manipulating more or less adroitly manufactured figures who are ultimately boring. Pinter, however, manages to escape this trap. Teddy, for example, the oldest brother in *The Homecoming,* hardly intelligible when approached conventionally, is nonetheless dramatically effective. At the climax of the play he stands quietly by while his wife is handled sexually by his brothers and later calmly conveys to her the family's invitation that she stay on with them in England and become a prostitute. Although it has been ingeniously suggested that Teddy's actions are explicable because he knows his family's tendencies and is therefore not surprised by them,[4] the validity of this argument is dubious. The most knowledgeable of sons would hardly be quite so *dégagé,* nor would he abet his family's proposal or his wife's compliance.[5] In fact, no amount of well intentioned argument will make Teddy's conduct psychologically comprehensible, because it is not. Yet, one must recognize that Teddy—who has withdrawn from the violent, passionate life of his family to the arid deserts (as his wife sees them) of America, who writes his critical works and maintains "intellectual equilibrium" —is not only a symbolic embodiment of emotional disengagement, of withdrawal into a world of intellect, but a disturbing dramatic personage. His dissociation from the climactic events of the play, grotesque psychologically, is the necessary action of a symbolic entity; yet at the same time he is very far indeed from resembling those magnificent caricatures of Ben Jonson whose monomania spurts from every line. As he speaks to his wife in his first scene, he

[4] See Esslin, p. 159.

[5] Pinter's comment, that Teddy leaves because he wants to avoid a "messy fight" and his marriage is breaking up anyway, is not necessarily disingenuous, though it may be mischievous. In any case, it suggests the proper distance between the author and the explicator, which Pinter has always been careful to maintain. See *Saturday Review,* April 8, 1967, pp. 56–58.

seems no more than a man reasonably nervous at seeing his home, and especially his father, after a six-year absence: ". . . he'll get a surprise in the morning, won't he? The old man. I think you'll like him very much. Honestly. He's a . . . well, he's old, of course. Getting on. *Pause.* I was born here, do you realize that?" One of Pinter's most notable skills is the ability not merely to catch the naturalistic note as he does here but to add to it as the play develops suggestive symbolic overtones that give it greater resonance and at certain climactic moments to intensify, even to alter it, so that character becomes symbol and the work moves into another dimension.

Pinter's plays require of their audiences a sensitivity to these shifts in aesthetic key—some slight, some abrupt and daring—and especially to those moments of symbolic expansion when the characters lunge forward, thrusting their significance at the beholder. The feeling of dislocation that the audience experiences as the plays move back and forth between the realistic psychological mode and the symbolic one accounts, in considerable part, for the sense of menace that pervades Pinter's world. But it is the threat of meaning rather than the threat of violence that lies at the root of Pinter's menace. The beatings, blackouts, and guns of the early plays are ultimately no more disquieting than the inner disturbances of the later ones. What is evoked by the comparatively crude, though brilliantly effective, devices of *The Room, The Dumb Waiter,* and *The Birthday Party* is the same thing that is suggested by the more subtle effects of the plays that follow: the fear that what lurks in the inner self will force us to acknowledge its presence. The result is that when audiences begin to hear the symbolic resonances of the plays, they also begin to feel the special menacing unease characteristic of them. For that sense of menace is intimately connected with a paradoxical phenomenon: the further the plays move into the symbolic realm, the nearer they come to the world of the audience itself.

In *The Dumb Waiter,* for example, the moment at which the dumb waiter begins to demand exotic dishes from the two gunmen (Ben's desperate explanations have for a few minutes staved off our apprehensions at its first requests) marks the shift from the realistic, if sinister, world of the two agents on a job to the symbolic one of two guilty creatures threatened by the demands of an unreasonable, infinitely powerful force, which they can only attempt to placate.

The audience feels the sense of menace not only from the threat of violence to the two characters on stage but from the sudden alteration of judgments and expectations as the play moves from the realistic mode to the symbolic. The mere fact of this shift is disturbing, for the subtle readjustment of aesthetic equilibrium forces us to recognize that something which had seemed secure—our relationship to the world of the play—is not. Moreover, up to this point we have seen the action as concerning, that is to say *confined,* to a pair of very special, even exotic, persons. But as we sense that the action is of wider scope, we are faced by the painful fact that we may be—as indeed we are—by implication included in it. The mere possibility is threatening. How much more threatening is it when we recognize that the symbolic world of this play—unlike its realistic one of gunmen, killings, and secret messages, which is quite foreign to most of us—is in fact the one we all inhabit in our daily existences. None of us is without guilt, and none of us is without the sense that unreasonable demands are being made upon us by forces and circumstances that we cannot fully understand.

At other moments in Pinter's work the sense of menace may be induced far more subtly than it is here, even by a mere shading of language, but it still derives from the symbolic evocation of some powerful threatening force. The short experimental play *Landscape* is probably Pinter's quietest work, consisting as it does entirely of two alternating monologues, one of them an interior meditation. At one point in the play the husband, Duff, who has been telling a rambling anecdote concerning a man who complained about the quality of the beer in a pub, explains how he triumphed over the complainer by a display of superior knowledge. As he speaks, his language, which has been restrained and commonplace, suddenly opens up to acquire poetic force and symbolic suggestiveness:

> This fellow knew bugger all about beer. He didn't know I'd been trained as a cellarman. That's why I could speak with authority. . . . A cellarman is the man responsible. He's the earliest up in the morning. Give the drayman a hand with the barrels. Down the slide through the cellarflaps. Lower them by rope to the racks. Rock them on the belly, put a rim up them, use balance and leverage, hike them up onto the racks. . . . The bung is on the vertical, in the bunghole. Spile the bung. Hammer the spile through the centre of the bung. That lets the

air through the bung, down the bunghole, lets the beer breathe. [Ellipsis marks indicate interruptions by the wife, Beth, here deleted.]

The concentrated images of masculine force and violent physical activity take this speech out of the realm of realistic conversation and give it thematic power. Since the central conflict of the play is between Beth's vision of peace, beauty, and fulfillment, associated with her lover and the beach, and Duff's altogether coarser, rougher, more sensual presence, the speech in effect brings this opposition into focus. In a later speech Duff describes an imagined scene in which he takes his wife sexually by force, but even in this earlier one there is much that evokes the violent, frustrated sexuality that is part of his significance: "Rock them on the belly, put a rim up them. . . . Hammer the spile through the centre of the bung. . . . down the bunghole." The multiplying implications of the word *bung* (stopper, anus, bruising force) combine with its heavy, obsessive repetitions (five times in these few lines) to create an exceptionally effective image of sexual violence. The carefully controlled patterns of assonance and alliteration also contribute, with rhythm and weight that are very far from the ramblings of ordinary conversation: "drayman . . . hand . . . barrels . . . slide . . . cellar-flaps. Lower . . . rope . . . racks. Rock . . . rim. . . ." Although Pinter is at the same time a master of suspenseful action, his achievements as a stylist give the plays an immediately recognizable identity. Out of the shabby materials of modern life and modern speech he creates a genuinely poetic drama—that is to say, one in which the meaning and the aesthetic effect are intimately related to the evocative power of words.

Initially, Pinter's special talent as a writer of dialogue seemed to be his ability to make effective stage speech out of the stumbling repetitions of semiliterate people, but from the first he has had a taste for exuberant rhetoric as well. (Despite its stark rhythms, the images of Bert Hudd's speech in *The Room,* as he describes himself driving his van, have some of the metaphorical power of Duff's: "I caned her along. She was good. . . . She went with me. She don't mix it with me. I use my hand. Like that. I get hold of her. . . .") An actor himself, Pinter is not afraid to give his players brilliant set pieces that demand the virtuosity and verbal control of Shakespearean verse speaking. Goldberg's supremely vulgar maunderings in *The Birthday Party,* for example, are of this order. At the climax of one of his reminiscences he says: "Humming away I'd be, past the children's playground. I'd tip my hat to the toddlers, I'd give a helping hand to a couple of stray dogs, everything came natural. I can see it like yesterday. The sun falling behind the dog stadium. Ah!" The grotesquerie of extending "a helping hand" to dogs rather than aged people and the intrusion of the dog stadium into what should be a description, however trite, of a natural scene raises the speech to a whimsically sinister parody of the idea that "everything came natural."

A closely related speech, in which the verbal debris of the commercial world is used as a weapon of attack, occurs near the beginning of the second act of *The Caretaker.* Mick is teasing Davies, the desperate and shabby tramp he has found in his house, by alternately abusing him, threatening him with arrest, and offering him ever more exorbitant and complicated arrangements for leasing part of the house. At the climax of the speech Mick's language soars beyond the colloquial and the psychologically appropriate into a violent outflooding of business jargon:

> On the other hand, if you prefer to approach it in the long-term way I know an insurance firm in West Ham'll be pleased to handle the deal for you. No strings attached, open and above board, untarnished record; twenty per cent interest, fifty per cent deposit; down payments, back payments, family allowances, bonus schemes, remission of term for good behaviour, six months lease, yearly examination of the relevant archives, tea laid on, disposal of shares, benefit extension, compensation on cessation, comprehensive indemnity against Riot, Civil Commotion, Labour Disturbances, Storm, Tempest, Thunderbolt, Larceny or Cattle all subject to a daily check and double check.

The piling up of the dehumanized verbiage of commercial contracts helps create part of the symbolic meaning of Mick's character (it is he who tempts Davies to betray his benefactor with a decorator's slick vision of modern luxury); as it continues in a spate of terms drawn from prison life and boarding houses, it further suggests the omnipresence of the institutional and materialistic, at once the elements of Mick's world and his ironic weapons against the broken, destitute Davies. In a last burst of linguistic aggression, he tells the wretched Davies that before any arrangements can be made he must produce a statement from his "personal medical attendant" that he has "the requisite fitness to carry the can." The abrupt shift from the commercial-legal pretentiousness of "personal medical attendant" and "requisite fitness" to the colloquial brutality of "carry the can" speaks volumes. Near this point Aston enters the room and the dialogue suddenly shifts again. The flood of words ceases and is replaced by silences, pauses, and commonplace fragments trembling on the verge of dissociation:

> *Silence.*
>
> *A drip sounds in the bucket* [hanging from the ceiling]. *They all look up.*
>
> *Silence.*
>
> *Mick.* You still got that leak.
>
> *Aston.* Yes.
>
> *Pause.*
>
> It's coming from the roof.
>
> *Mick.* From the roof, eh?
>
> *Aston.* Yes.
>
> *Pause.*
>
> I'll have to tar it over.
>
> *Mick.* You're going to tar it over?
>
> *Aston.* Yes.
>
> *Mick.* What?
>
> *Aston.* The cracks.
>
> *Pause.*
>
> *Mick.* You'll be tarring over the cracks on the roof.
>
> *Aston.* Yes.
>
> *Pause.*

This passage, in its way as highly stylized as Mick's outburst, does more than make a striking theatrical contrast. By spacing out the lines and removing most of the significant meaning from them, Pinter focuses almost our entire attention on what is not said, what cannot be said, though it is apparent in the situation: Davies' terror and befuddlement, Aston's almost catatonic remoteness, and Mick's sudden loss of power as Aston's presence prevents his continuing to dominate and torment Davies. Although here, as elsewhere in Pinter, the silences and the rambling phrases are designed to allow the submerged material of the scene to rise to the surface, the lines themselves carry hints and suggestions. In the idea of putting one's house in order Pinter has recognized a traditional metaphor for putting one's life in order, an action these characters notably fail to perform. Moreover, the inanities of the dialogue produce enough laughter to ease the tension of the scene and distance the audience slightly from the action. For all their ultimate grimness, Pinter's plays have a severe humor, a part of their appeal, that testifies to his delicate control.

III.

All of the points so far commented on are aspects of Pinter's style; they are the immediate, observable qualities that give to his plays their characteristic identity. To borrow Stanley's phrase from *The Birthday Party,* they reveal a "unique touch, absolutely unique." But these qualities—the mysterious difficulty in verifying events; the apparently bizarre behavior of characters, who shift back and forth between psychological and symbolic modes; the pervasive sense of menace; the silences and other distinctive verbal traits—though they are all significant devices for conveying Pinter's vision, are not the substance of what is conveyed. They are means rather than ends. They are ways of directing our attention to the area under the cocktail cabinet where the weasel is lurking.

To get a clearer view of the beast and a fuller understanding of its nature one must also consider the materials of which the plays are made: the settings, the kinds of personages, the patterns of action. The most immediately observable motif in Pinter's work is his characteristic setting, the room. He himself noted in an interview that the generating experience for several of his plays was seeing people enclosed in a room with each other:

> I went into a room and saw one person standing up and one person sitting down, and a few weeks later I wrote *The Room.* I went into another room and saw two people sitting down, and a few years later I wrote *The Birthday Party.* I looked through a door into a third room, and saw two people standing up and I wrote *The Caretaker.*[6]

Despite its whimsical severity, Pinter's comment suggests why these circumstances had so much appeal for him. The room becomes for Pinter a way of blocking out the diffuse claims of the external

[6] "Writing for Myself" (An Interview with Richard Findlater), *Twentieth Century,* CLXIC (February 1961), 174.

world and concentrating on the central facts of existence as he conceives of them. Most modern plays, simply because they reflect modern life, do indeed take place in rooms; and occasionally the room itself becomes a significant element in the scheme of the play, as in Sartre's *No Exit,* where the room in hell that confines the characters images the forces that lock us into identities and relationships that are tormenting in life. This room may well have been a momentary convenience for Sartre, but in Pinter's work the room repeatedly, almost regularly, becomes a crucial element: a place of shelter, a refuge tenuously maintained against the assaults of the outside world, in which the entrance or exit of any character and the resulting shift in relations is a matter of the utmost consequence. Pinter's first words as a playwright in the significantly titled *The Room* are a rambling monologue about the safety of a room and the dangers outside it: "No, this room's all right for me. I mean, you know where you are. . . . This is a good room. You've got a chance in a place like this." From these initial phrases the theme has run through Pinter's work, with all of his major plays, the four full-length stage pieces, offering one variation or another on it. In *The Birthday Party* Stanley has retreated to the shelter of the boarding-house into which Goldberg and McCann pursue him; Aston, in *The Caretaker,* has largely retired to the room into which he brings Davies; Teddy and Ruth intrude into the confines of Teddy's family in *The Homecoming*; and in what is at the time of this writing Pinter's latest play, *Old Times,* Anna enters the secluded household of Deeley and Kate to struggle for a position of dominance.

The invasion of a room, then, is the central action in each of Pinter's major plays. But the room is less important as an architectural feature than as a means of delineating a state of mind. The household that the room shelters, one person or several, presents a body of feelings and attitudes that give both it and the room a special emotional identity. Not only is the room itself conceived of as a refuge, but those who have withdrawn to it enter into a state of inaction that involves the denial of some aspect of existence. Through fear or incapacity or trauma they have cut themselves off from some vital part of life—family relations, competitive striving, sexuality—and lead a safe but limited existence in a sheltered but confined area. Thus Stanley's retreat is from his family and his home, as well as from some nameless organization he is said to have betrayed, into a world of inaction and infantile, Oedipal sexuality. Aston's withdrawal is from a world that has denied his message and tormented him; Kate's is from her sexual past. The family world of *The Homecoming* has put behind it everything but aggression and appetite.

If the motif of the room is recognized as a means of projecting in dramatic terms the theme of inaction and withdrawal, then the lesser plays orbiting about the major ones are seen to be following recognizable paths. Some of these plays—notably *The Room* and *The Basement*—involve rooms directly; almost all deal with the passivity that Pinter often uses a room to express. Such is the state of Edward, in *A Slight Ache,* who has retired to his elegant house to write "theological and philosophical essays" (anticipations of Teddy's "critical works" in *The Homecoming*). *The Lover* and *The Collection,* closely related plays, both concern a woman for whom a conventional marriage involves withdrawal from a satisfyingly vital sexual life. In *The Lover* she alleviates this state with the help of her husband, who shares her feelings and willingly takes the part of a fantasy lover; in *The Collection* she creates the fantasy lover herself—out of a conversation with a young homosexual—and then stimulates her husband by telling him of his supposed rival. The two brief experimental plays, *Landscape* and *Silence,* also each center on a woman, withdrawn from life into age and remoteness, who meditates on the two men she has known. In each case one of the men is more sensitive, comparatively quiescent, the other rougher, more sensual.

These oppositions persist throughout most of Pinter's work. If his rooms tend to enclose worlds characterized by retreat and inaction, by passivity and sexlessness, then the powers that intrude upon them are usually vital and sinister, potent and cruel. Recognizing their interplay, we recognize one source of Pinter's mysteriousness; for ambiguity is always mysterious, and between such alternatives no clear choice is possible. The disintegrating lassitude that Stanley has lapsed into at the beginning of *The Birthday Party* is hardly preferable to the bumptious certainties and brutish sentimentality of Goldberg and McCann: to be rescued from apathy is to be destroyed by vitality. Inevitably, the very forces that draw one forth from retreat and safety, childishness and inaction, are the forces of hope, lust, will to action and power from which one has hidden. In the final analysis these opposing tendencies are mighty opposites of the inner self, locked in eternal conflict. Though they are not to be equated with the id and the superego (the latter is too rational and moral for Pinter's vision, the former too merely emotive), like those extremes of the self they are necessarily linked together: extensions, as it were, from a common center. Because the human temperament embraces both these extremes, the qualities interpenetrate in the play. Stanley has his cruelties just as Goldberg has his weaknesses. But Goldberg can give vulgar expression to the very qualities that Stanley has repressed, sexuality and aggressive dominance.

In the Pinter world, where apathy and vitality are linked in conflict, the urge to dominance often leads to a dubious triumph. When Davies must make the doubtful choice between the inhuman lassitude of Aston and the shabby, worldly energy of Mick, the impulse to dominate leads him to think he can ally himself with Mick and have power, when his only hope lies in refuge with Aston. For power in the world of Pinter's dramas is not to be possessed by reaching for it. Power is the prerogative of those who have vital energy. Her position as a desired sexual object gives Ruth of *The Homecoming* her triumphant status at the end of that play. In *The Dumb Waiter,* a study in dominance, Ben's alliance with the authority of the waiter itself gives him power over Gus.

Although refuge and intrusion, apathy and vitality, dominance and submission are among the materials that Pinter works with, no general terms should be applied mechanically to specific plays. Not all women are monsters of sexual power; not all rooms are refuges. The struggle for dominance, for example, only appears tangentially in *Landscape* and not at all in *Silence* but returns with insidious force in *Old Times.* Moreover, Pinter's vision is not necessarily as anarchic as these comments might suggest. There is inherent in his work a quite traditional moral judgment recognizing that the clashes of these antipathies produce human cruelty and destructiveness, though no recipes or even hopes for improvement are offered. The clarity of vision with which Davies is seen and judged in *The Caretaker* is only the most obvious case in point. As always, in approaching a complex and subtle writer, one must tread lightly and discreetly. Pinter is neither a theatrical trickster nor an abstruse metaphysician; he is an artist whose special style expresses his meaning, whose subject is a significant part of human experience.

IV.

These introductory comments, though meant to suggest the particular character of Pinter's style and some of the materials with which he works, are no substitute for detailed consideration of individual plays and recurring themes. This function the articles brought together on the following pages are intended to perform. They have been chosen for their interest and not because they develop any single coherent view of Pinter. Indeed, the diversity—even the contradictions—of points of view thus achieved is one of the virtues of this kind of volume. Two attitudes which have upon occasion been seriously maintained—on the one hand that Pinter is a mere manipulator of dramatic effect and on the other that he is so profound as to be unintelligible—are for obvious reasons not represented here, but others collide randomly as the essays trace the course of his career. Not only do the articles follow, insofar as possible, the chronology of Pinter's plays, but in doing so they follow, roughly, the sequence in which these studies were written. Thus the reader who chooses to take them in this order will be tracing both the development of Pinter's art and our understanding of it.

The first three articles constitute an exception. Though Pinter consistently, and rightly, refuses to interpret his plays, he has spoken frankly on the process of their creation, on the influences that have shaped his work, and on the themes that he himself feels are paramount. The personal interview that opens this volume has thus a special authority. Since the next two articles both deal with aspects of Pinter's language and technique, they too are not limited by chronology. Ranging generally over the plays, they make up a convenient introductory group. Martin Esslin's "Language and Silence" concentrates on Pinter's language, showing through precise analysis of a wide range of examples how he makes such devices as repetition, association, shifts in levels of diction, and pauses and silences into an expressive linguistic style. John Lahr, in "Pinter and Chekhov:

The Bond of Naturalism," is primarily concerned with differences in the two playwrights' views of nature: the contrast between the world of nature in Chekhov, which offers at least a significant comment on human failings, and the squalid, indifferent urban universe of Pinter, marking, Lahr suggests, a crucial shift from a Victorian to a modern consciousness.

The earliest of the essays on specific plays is Valerie Minogue's "Taking Care of the Caretaker." Rejecting the initial critical emphasis on Pinter's use of lower-class idiom, she points out that the central circumstances and behavior patterns of *The Caretaker* reflect the familiar, universal exigencies of human life. In "The World of Harold Pinter" Ruby Cohn underscores Pinter's allegiance not only to the metaphysical despair of Samuel Beckett but to the social rage of John Osborne and the Angry Young Men of England's postwar generation of playwrights. She traces through the plays, from *The Room* to *The Caretaker,* the theme of the destruction of a more or less pathetic hero by a social-religious "System" that shows its victims no mercy. James T. Boulton, on the other hand, in "Harold Pinter: *The Caretaker* and Other Plays" contrasts Pinter with Osborne, whose coherent rhetoric and explicit motivation of character create a reasonable and comprehensible stage world quite different from the mysterious, secluded rooms of Pinter's. For Boulton, Pinter's characters, haunted by a nostalgia for the lost security of childhood, are universal symbols of loneliness and fear. The section of John Russell Taylor's "A Room and Some Views: Harold Pinter" here reprinted is especially helpful since it discusses not only *The Caretaker* but the considerable number of radio and television plays (such as *The Dwarfs, The Collection,* and *The Lover*) that Pinter wrote between that play and *The Homecoming.* With sympathy and good sense Taylor shows how the question of verification, posed for the audience by the early works, becomes in Pinter's "realistic" phrase a problem for the characters themselves.

John Pesta's "Pinter's Usurpers" carries his study of Pinter's works through *The Homecoming* to include the screenplay of *The Servant.* Tracing a pattern of usurpation in Pinter's work, he notes that the usurpers are often ambiguous figures, sometimes aggressive, sometimes insecure. A quite different view is argued by R. F. Storch in "Harold Pinter's Happy Families," where the emphasis is placed not on the usurpation but on the sheltering area, the family, with its "primitive fears" and "regressive fantasies." Bert O. States, in "Pinter's *Homecoming*: The Shock of Nonrecognition," maintains in a lively and ingenious argument that critical analysis in terms of psychological motivation or mythic patterning is irrelevant to *The Homecoming* and that both the author and his characters are to be understood as ironists, playing with violence and evil from a detached, aesthetic standpoint. In this volume's concluding essay the editor presents an opposed, perhaps less forbidding, argument, suggesting that Pinter's plays are concerned with a central human issue, the conflict in the inner self between a dangerous vitality and a restraining apathy. The development of this theme is traced through Pinter's most recent plays: *Landscape, Silence,* and *Old Times.*

Harold Pinter: An Interview

INTERVIEWER. When did you start writing plays, and why?

PINTER. My first play was *The Room,* written when I was twenty-seven. A friend of mine called Henry Woolf was a student in the drama department at Bristol University at the time when it was the only drama department in the country. He had the opportunity to direct a play, and as he was my oldest friend he knew I'd been writing, and he knew I had an idea for a play, though I hadn't written any of it. I was acting in Rep at the time, and he told me he had to have the play the next week to meet his schedule. I said this was ridiculous, he might get it in six months. And then I wrote it in four days.

INTERVIEWER. Has writing always been so easy for you?

PINTER. Well, I had been writing for years, hundreds of poems and short pieces of prose. About a dozen had been published in little magazines. I wrote a novel as well; it's not good enough to be published, really, and never has been. After I wrote *The Room,* which I didn't see performed for a few weeks, I started to work immediately on *The Birthday Party.*

INTERVIEWER. What led you to do that so quickly?

PINTER. It was the process of writing a play which had started me going. Then I went to see *The Room,* which was a remarkable experience. Since I'd never written a play before, I'd of course never seen one of mine performed, never had an audience sitting there. The only people who'd ever seen what I'd written had been a few friends and my wife. So to sit in the audience—well, I wanted to piss very badly throughout the whole thing, and at the end I dashed out behind the bicycle shed. . . .

INTERVIEWER. What other effect did contact with an audience have on you?

"Harold Pinter: An Interview" (with Lawrence M. Bensky). From *Writers at Work: The Paris Review Interviews, Third Series,* edited by George Plimpton.

PINTER. I was very encouraged by the response of that university audience, though no matter what the response had been I would have written *The Birthday Party,* I know that. Watching first nights, though I've seen quite a few by now, is never any better. It's a nerve-wracking experience. It's not a question of whether the play goes well or badly. It's not the audience reaction, it's *my* reaction. I'm rather hostile toward audiences —I don't much care for large bodies of people collected together. Everyone knows that audiences vary enormously, it's a mistake to care too much about them. The thing one should be concerned with is whether the performance has expressed what one set out to express in writing the play. It sometimes does.

INTERVIEWER. Do you think that without the impetus provided by your friend at Bristol you would have gotten down to writing plays?

PINTER. Yes, I think I was going to write *The Room.* I just wrote it a bit quicker under the circumstances, he just triggered something off. *The Birthday Party* had also been in my mind for a long time. It was sparked off from a very distinct situation in digs when I was on tour. In fact the other day a friend of mine gave me a letter I wrote to him in nineteen-fifty something, Christ knows when it was. This is what it says, "I have filthy insane digs, a great bulging scrag of a woman with breasts rolling at her belly, an obscene household, cats, dogs, filth, teastrainers, mess, oh bullocks, talk, chat rubbish shit scratch dung poison, infantility, deficient order in the upper fretwork, fucking roll on . . ." Now the thing about this is *that* was *The Birthday Party*—I was in those digs, and this woman was Meg in the play, and there was a fellow staying there in Eastbourne, on the coast. The whole thing remained with me, and three years later I wrote the play.

INTERVIEWER. Why wasn't there a character representing you in the play?

PINTER. I had—I have—nothing to say about myself, directly. I wouldn't know where to begin. Particularly since I often look at myself in the mirror and say, "Who the hell's that?"

INTERVIEWER. And you don't think being represented as a character on stage would help you find out?

PINTER. No.

INTERVIEWER. Have your plays usually been drawn from situations you've been in? *The Caretaker,* for example.

PINTER. I'd met a few, quite a few, tramps—you know, just in the normal course of events, and I think there was one particular one . . . I didn't know him very well, he did most of the talking when I saw him. I bumped into him a few times, and about a year or so afterward he sparked this thing off. . . .

INTERVIEWER. Had it occurred to you to act in *The Room*?

PINTER. No, no—the acting was a separate activity altogether. Though I wrote *The Room, The Birthday Party,* and *The Dumb Waiter* in 1957, I was acting all the time in a repertory company, doing all kinds of jobs, traveling to Bournemouth and Torquay and Birmingham. I finished *The Birthday Party* while I was touring in some kind of farce, I don't remember the name.

INTERVIEWER. As an actor, do you find yourself with a compelling sense of how roles in your plays should be performed?

PINTER. Quite often I have a compelling sense of how a role should be played. And I'm proved—equally as often—quite wrong.

INTERVIEWER. Do you see yourself in each role as you write? And does your acting help you as a playwright?

PINTER. I read them all aloud to myself while writing. But I don't see myself in each role—I couldn't play most of them. My acting doesn't impede my playwrighting because of these limitations. For example, I'd like to write a play—I've frequently thought of this—entirely about women.

INTERVIEWER. Your wife, Vivien Merchant, frequently appears in your plays. Do you write parts for her?

PINTER. No. I've never written any part for any actor, and the same applies to my wife. I just think she's a very good actress and a very interesting actress to work with, and I want her in my plays.

INTERVIEWER. Acting was your profession when you first started to write plays?

PINTER. Oh, yes, it was all I ever did. I didn't go to university. I left school at sixteen—I was fed up and restless. The only thing that interested me at school was English language and literature, but I didn't have Latin and so couldn't go on to university. So I went to a few drama schools, not studying seriously; I was mostly in love at the time and tied up with that.

INTERVIEWER. Were the drama schools of any use to you as a playwright?

PINTER. None whatsoever. It was just living.

INTERVIEWER. Did you go to a lot of plays in your youth?

PINTER. No, very few. The only person I really liked to see was Donald Wolfit in a Shakespearean Company at the time. I admired him tremendously; his Lear is still the best I've ever seen. And then I was reading, for years, a great deal of modern literature, mostly novels.

INTERVIEWER. No playwrights—Brecht, Pirandello . . .

PINTER. Oh certainly not, not for years. I read Hemingway, Dostoevski, Joyce and Henry Miller at a very early age, and Kafka. I'd read Beckett's novels, too, but I'd never heard of Ionesco until after I'd written the first few plays.

INTERVIEWER. Do you think these writers had any influence on your writing?

PINTER. I've been influenced *personally* by everyone I've ever read—and I read all the time—but none of these writers particularly influenced my writing. Beckett and Kafka stayed with me the most—I think Beckett is the best prose writer living. My world is still bound up by other writers —that's one of the best things in it.

INTERVIEWER. Has music influenced your writing, do you think?

PINTER. I don't know how music can influence writing; but it has been very important for me, both jazz and classical music. I feel a sense of music continually in writing, which is a different matter from having been influenced by it. Boulez and Webern are now composers I listen to a great deal.

INTERVIEWER. Do you get impatient with the limitations of writing for the theater?

PINTER. No. It's quite different; the theater's much the most difficult kind of writing for me, the most naked kind, you're so entirely restricted. I've done some film work, but for some reason or other I haven't found it very easy to satisfy myself on an original idea for a film. *Tea Party,* which I did for television, is actually a film, cinematic, I wrote it like that. Television and films are simpler than the theater—if you get tired of a scene you just drop it and go on to another one. (I'm exaggerating, of course.) What *is* so different about the stage is that you're just *there,* stuck—there are your characters stuck on the stage, you've got to live with them and deal with them. I'm not a very inventive writer in the sense of using the technical devices other playwrights do—look at Brecht! I can't use the stage the way he does, I just haven't got that kind of imagination, so I find myself stuck with these characters who are either sitting or standing, and they've either got to walk out of a door, or come in through a door, and that's about all they can do.

INTERVIEWER. And talk.

PINTER. Or keep silent.

INTERVIEWER. After *The Room,* what effect did the production of your next plays have on your writing?

PINTER. *The Birthday Party* was put on at the Lyric, Hammersmith in London. It went on a little tour of Oxford and Cambridge first, and was very successful. When it came to London it was completely massacred by the critics—absolutely slaughtered. I've never really known why, nor am I particularly interested. It ran a week. I've framed the statement of the box office takings: 260 pounds, including a first night of 140 pounds and the Thursday matinée of two pounds, nine shillings—there were six people there. I was completely new to writing for the professional theater, and it was rather a shock when it happened. But I went on writing—the BBC were very helpful. I wrote *A Slight Ache* on commission from them. In 1960 *The Dumb Waiter* was produced, and then *The Caretaker.* The only really bad experience I've had was *The Birthday Party;* I was so green and gauche—not that I'm rosy and confident now, but comparatively . . . Anyway, for things like stage design I didn't know how to cope, and I didn't know how to talk to the director.

INTERVIEWER. What was the effect of this adversity on you? How was it different from unfavorable criticism of your acting, which surely you'd had before?

PINTER. It was a great shock, and I was very depressed for about forty-eight hours. It was my wife, actually, who said just that to me, "You've had bad notices before," etc. There's no question but that her common sense and practical help got me over that depression, and I've never felt anything like that again.

INTERVIEWER. You've directed several of your plays. Will you continue to do so?

PINTER. No. I've come to think it's a mistake. I work much as I write, just moving from one thing to another to see what's going to happen next. One tries to get the thing . . . *true.* But I rarely get it. I think I'm more useful as the author closely involved with a play: as a director I think I tend to inhibit the actors, because however objective I am about the text and try not to insist that *this is what's meant,* I think there is an obligation on the actors too heavy to bear.

INTERVIEWER. Since you are an actor, do actors in your plays ever approach you and ask you to change lines or aspects of their roles?

PINTER. Sometimes, quite rarely, lines are changed when we're working together. I don't at all believe in the anarchic theater of so-called "creative" actors—the actors can do that in someone else's plays. Which wouldn't, however, at all affect their ability to play in mine.

INTERVIEWER. Which of your plays did you first direct?

PINTER. I co-directed *The Collection* with Peter Hall. And then I directed *The Lover* and *The Dwarfs* on the same bill at the Arts. *The Lover* didn't stand much of a chance because it was my decision, regretted by everyone—except me—to do *The Dwarfs,* which is apparently the most intractable, impossible piece of work. Apparently ninety-nine people out of a hundred feel it's a waste of time, and the audience hated it.

INTERVIEWER. It seems the densest of your plays in the sense that there's quite a bit of talk and very little action. Did this represent an experiment for you?

PINTER. No. The fact is that *The Dwarfs* came from my unpublished novel, which was written a long time ago. I took a great deal from it, particularly the kind of state of mind that the characters were in.

INTERVIEWER. So this circumstance of composition is not likely to be repeated?

PINTER. No. I should add that even though it is, as you say, more dense, it had great value, great interest for me. From my point of view, the general delirium and states of mind and reactions and relationships in the play—although terribly sparse—are clear to me. I know all the things that aren't said, and the way the characters actually look at each other, and what they mean by looking at each other. It's a play about betrayal and distrust. It does seem very confusing and obviously it can't be successful. But it was good for me to do.

INTERVIEWER. Is there more than one way to direct your play successfully?

PINTER. Oh, yes, but always around the same central truth of the play—if that's distorted, then it's bad. The main difference in interpretation comes from the actors. The director can certainly be responsible for a disaster, too—the first performance of *The Caretaker* in Germany was heavy and posturized. There's no blueprint for any play, and several have been done entirely successfully without me helping in the production at all.

INTERVIEWER. When you are working on one, what is the key to a good writer-director relationship?

PINTER. What is absolutely essential is avoiding all defensiveness between author and director. It's a matter of mutual trust and openness. If that isn't there, it's just a waste of time.

INTERVIEWER. Peter Hall, who has directed many of your plays, says that they rely on precise verbal form and rhythm, and when you write "pause" it means something other than "silence," and three dots are different from a full stop. Is his sensitivity to this kind of writing responsible for your working well together?

PINTER. Yes, it is, very much so. I do pay great attention to those points you just mentioned. Hall once held a dot and pause rehearsal for the actors in *The Homecoming*. Although it sounds bloody pretentious it was apparently very valuable.

INTERVIEWER. Do you outline plays before you start to write them?

PINTER. Not at all. I don't know what kind of characters my plays will have until they . . . well, until they *are*. Until they indicate to me what they are. I don't conceptualize in any way. Once I've got the clues I follow them—that's my job, really, to follow the clues.

INTERVIEWER. What do you mean by clues? Can you remember how one of your plays developed in your mind—or was it a line by line progression?

PINTER. Of course I can't remember exactly how a given play developed in my mind. I think what happens is that I write in a very high state of excitement and frustration. I follow what I see on the paper in front of me—one sentence after another. That doesn't mean I don't have a dim, possible overall idea—the image that starts off doesn't just engender what happens immediately, it engenders the possibility of an overall happening, which carries me through. I've got an idea of what *might* happen—sometimes I'm absolutely right, but on many occasions I've been proved wrong by what does actually happen. Sometimes I'm going along and I find myself writing "C. comes in" when I didn't know that he was going to come in; he *had* to come in at that point, that's all.

INTERVIEWER. In *The Homecoming*, Sam, a character who hasn't been very active for a while, suddenly cries out and collapses several minutes from the end of the play. Is this an example of what you mean? It seems abrupt.

PINTER. It suddenly seemed to me right. It just came. I knew he'd have to say something at one time in this section and this is what happened, that's what he said.

INTERVIEWER. Might characters therefore develop beyond your control of them, changing your idea—even if it's a vague idea—of what the play's about?

PINTER. I'm ultimately holding the ropes, so they never get too far away.

INTERVIEWER. Do you sense when you should bring down the curtain, or do you work the text consciously toward a moment you've already determined?

PINTER. It's pure instinct. The curtain comes down when the rhythm seems right—when the action calls for a finish. I'm very fond of curtain lines, of doing them properly.

INTERVIEWER. Do you feel your plays are therefore structurally successful? That you're able to communicate this instinct for rhythm to the play?

PINTER. No, not really, and that's my main concern, to get the structure right. I always write three drafts, but you have to leave it eventually. There comes a point when you say that's it, I can't do anything more. The only play which gets remotely near to a structural entity which satisfies me is *The Homecoming*. *The Birthday Party* and *The Caretaker* have too much writing . . . I want to iron it down, eliminate things. Too many words irritate me sometimes, but I can't help them, they just seem to come out—out of the fellow's mouth. I don't really examine my works too much, but I'm aware that quite often in what I write, some fellow at some point says an awful lot.

INTERVIEWER. Most people would agree that the strength in your plays lies in just this verbal aspect, the patterns and force of character you can get from it. Do you get these words from people you've heard talking—do you eavesdrop?

PINTER. I spend *no* time listening in that sense. Occasionally I hear something, as we all do, walking about. But the words come as I'm writing the characters, not before.

INTERVIEWER. Why do you think the conversations in your plays are so effective?

PINTER. I don't know, I think possibly it's because people fall back on anything they can lay their hands on verbally to keep away from the danger of knowing, and of being known.

INTERVIEWER. What areas in writing plays give you the most trouble?

PINTER. They're all so inextricably interrelated I couldn't possibly judge.

INTERVIEWER. Several years ago, *Encounter* had an extensive series of quotations from people in the arts about the advisability of Britain joining the Common Market. Your statement was the shortest anyone made, "I have no interest in the matter and do not care what happens." Does this sum up your feeling about politics, or current affairs?

PINTER. Not really. Though that's exactly what I feel about the Common Market—I just don't care a damn about the Common Market. But it isn't quite true to say that I'm in any way indifferent to current affairs. I'm in the normal state of being very confused—uncertain, irritated, and indignant in turns, sometimes indifferent. Generally I try to get on with what I can do and leave it at that. I don't think I've got any kind of social function that's of any value, and politically there's no question of my getting involved because the issues are by no means simple—to be a politician you have to be able to present a simple picture even if you don't see things that way.

INTERVIEWER. Has it ever occurred to you to express political opinions through your characters?

PINTER. No. Ultimately, politics do bore me, though I recognize they are responsible for a good deal of suffering. I distrust ideological statements of any kind.

INTERVIEWER. But do you think that the picture of personal threat which is sometimes presented on your stage is troubling in a larger sense, a political sense, or doesn't this have any relevance?

PINTER. I don't feel myself threatened by *any* political body or activity at all. I like living in England. I don't care about political structures—they don't alarm me, but they cause a great deal of suffering to millions of people.

I'll tell you what I really think about politicians. The other night I watched some politicians on television talking about Vietnam. I wanted very much to burst through the screen with a flame-thrower and burn their eyes out and their balls off and then inquire from them how they would assess this action from a political point of view.

INTERVIEWER. Would you ever use this anger in a politically-oriented play?

PINTER. I have occasionally out of irritation thought about writing a play with a satirical point. I once did, actually, a play that no one knows about. A full-length play written after *The Caretaker*. Wrote the whole damn thing in three drafts. It was called *The Hothouse* and was about an institution in which patients were kept: all that was presented was the hierarchy, the people who ran the institution; one never knew what happened to the patients or what they were there for or who they were. It was heavily satirical and it was quite useless. I never began to like any of the characters, they really didn't live at all. So I discarded the play at once. The characters were so purely cardboard. I was intentionally—for the only time, I think—trying to make a point, an explicit point, that these were nasty people and I disapproved of them. And therefore they didn't begin to live. Whereas in other plays of mine every single character, even a bastard like Goldberg in *The Birthday Party,* I care for.

INTERVIEWER. You often speak of your characters as living beings. Do they become so after you've written a play? While you're writing it?

PINTER. Both.

INTERVIEWER. As real as people you know?

PINTER. No, but different. I had a terrible dream, after I'd written *The Caretaker,* about the two brothers. My house burned down in the dream, and I tried to find out who was responsible. I was led through all sorts of alleys and cafés and eventually I arrived at an inner room somewhere and there were the two brothers from the play. And I said, so you burned down my house. They said don't be too worried about it, and I said I've got everything in there, everything, you don't realize what you've done, and they said it's all right, we'll compensate you for it, we'll look after you all right—the younger brother was talking—and thereupon I wrote them out a check for fifty quid . . . *I* gave *them* a check for fifty quid!

INTERVIEWER. Do you have a particular interest in psychology?

PINTER. No.

INTERVIEWER. None at all? Did you have some purpose in mind in writing the speech where the older brother describes his troubles in a mental hospital at the end of Act II in *The Caretaker*?

PINTER. Well, I had a purpose in the sense that Aston suddenly opened his mouth. My purpose was to let him go on talking until he was finished and then . . . bring the curtain down. I had no ax to grind there. And the one thing that people have missed is that it isn't necessary to conclude that everything Aston says about his experiences in the mental hospital is true.

INTERVIEWER. There's a sense of terror and a threat of violence in most of your plays. Do you see the world as an essentially violent place?

PINTER. The world *is* a pretty violent place, it's as simple as that, so any violence in the plays comes out quite naturally. It seems to me an essential and inevitable factor.

I think what you're talking about began in *The Dumb Waiter,* which from my point of view is a relatively simple piece of work. The violence is really only an expression of the question of dominance and subservience, which is possibly a repeated theme in my plays. I wrote a short story a long time ago called "The Examination," and my ideas of violence carried on from there. That short story dealt very explicitly with two people in one room having a battle of an unspecified nature, in which the question was one of who was dominant at what point and how they were going to be dominant and what tools they would use to achieve dominance and how they would try to undermine the other person's dominance. A threat is constantly there: it's got to do with this question of being in the uppermost position, or attempting to be. That's something of what attracted me to do the screenplay of *The Servant,* which was someone else's story, you know. I wouldn't call this violence so much as a battle for positions, it's a very common, everyday thing.

INTERVIEWER. Do these ideas of everyday battles, or of violence, come from any experiences you've had yourself?

PINTER. Everyone encounters violence in some way or other. It so happens I did encounter it in quite an extreme form after the war, in the East End, when the Fascists were coming back to life in England. I got into quite a few fights down there. If you looked remotely like a Jew you might be in trouble. Also, I went to a Jewish club, by an old railway arch, and there were quite a lot of people often waiting with broken milk bottles in a particular alley we used to walk through. There were one or two ways of getting out of it—one was a purely physical way, of course, but you couldn't do anything about the milk bottles—*we* didn't have any milk bottles. The best way was to talk to them, you know, sort of "Are you all right?" "Yes, I'm all right." "Well, that's all right then, isn't it?" And all the time keep walking toward the lights of the main road.

Another thing: we were often taken for communists. If you went by, or happened to be passing, a Fascist's street meeting, and looked in any way antagonistic—this was in Ridley Road market, near Dalston Junction—they'd interpret your very being, especially if you had books under your arms, as evidence of your being a communist. There was a good deal of violence there, in those days.

INTERVIEWER. Did this lead you toward some kind of pacifism?

PINTER. I was fifteen when the war ended. There was never any question of my going when I was called up for military service three years later: I couldn't see any point in it at all. I refused to go. So I was taken in a police car to the medical examination. Then I had two tribunals and two trials. I could have gone to prison—I took my toothbrush to the trials—but it so happened that the magistrate was slightly sympathetic, so I was fined instead, thirty pounds in all. Perhaps I'll be called up again in the next war, but I won't go.

INTERVIEWER. Robert Brustein has said of modern drama, "The rebel dramatist becomes an evangelist proselytizing for his faith." Do you see yourself in that role?

PINTER. I don't know what he's talking about. I don't know for what faith I could possibly be proselytizing.

INTERVIEWER. The theater is a very competitive business. Are you, as a writer, conscious of competing against other playwrights?

PINTER. Good writing excites me, and makes life worth living. I'm never conscious of any competition going on here.

INTERVIEWER. Do you read things written about you?

PINTER. Yes. Most of the time I don't know what they're talking about; I don't really read them all the way through. Or I read it and it goes —if you asked me what had been said, I would have very little idea. But there are exceptions, mainly nonprofessional critics.

INTERVIEWER. How much are you aware of an audience when you write?

PINTER. Not very much. But I'm aware that this is a public medium. I don't want to *bore* the audience, I want to keep them glued to what happens. So I try to write as *exactly* as possible. I would try to do that anyway, audience or no audience.

INTERVIEWER. There is a story—mentioned by Brustein in the *The Theater of Revolt*—that Ionesco once left a performance of Genet's *The Blacks* because he felt he was being attacked, and the actors were enjoying it. Would you ever hope for a similar reaction in your audience? Would you react this way yourself?

PINTER. I've had that reaction—it's happened to me recently here in London, when I went to see *US*, the Royal Shakespeare Company's anti-Vietnam war production. There was a kind of attack—I don't like being subjected to propaganda, and I detest soapboxes. I want to present things clearly in my own plays, and sometimes this does make an audience very uncomfortable, but there's no question about causing offense for its own sake.

INTERVIEWER. Do you therefore feel the play failed to achieve its purpose —inspiring opposition to the war?

PINTER. Certainly. The chasm between the reality of the war in Vietnam and the image of what *US* presented on the stage was so enormous as to be quite preposterous. If it was meant to lecture or shock the audience I think it was most presumptuous. It's impossible to make a major theatrical statement about such a matter when television and the press have made everything so clear.

INTERVIEWER. Do you consciously make crisis situations humorous? Often an audience at your plays finds its laughter turning against itself as it realizes what the situation in the play actually is.

PINTER. Yes, that's very true, yes. I'm rarely consciously writing humor, but sometimes I find myself laughing at some particular point which has suddenly struck me as being funny. I agree that more often than not the speech only *seems* to be funny—the man in question is actually fighting a battle for his life.

INTERVIEWER. There are sexual undertones in many of these crisis situations, aren't there? How do you see the use of sex in the theater today?

PINTER. I do object to one thing to do with sex: this scheme afoot on the part of many "liberal-minded" persons to open up obscene language to general commerce. It should be the dark secret language of the underworld. There are very few words—you shouldn't kill them by overuse. I have used such words once or twice in my plays, but I couldn't get them through the Lord Chamberlain. They're great, wonderful words, but must be used very sparingly. The pure publicity of freedom of language fatigues me, because it's a demonstration rather than something said.

INTERVIEWER. Do you think you've inspired any imitations? Have you ever seen anything in a film or theater which struck you as, well, Pinteresque?

PINTER. That word! These damn words and that word Pinteresque particularly—I don't know what they're bloody well talking about! I think it's a great burden for me to carry, and for other writers to carry . . . Oh, very occasionally I've thought listening to something, hello, that rings a bell, but it goes no further than that. I really do think that writers write on . . . just write, and I find it difficult to believe I'm any kind of influence on other writers. I've seen very little evidence of it, anyway; other people seem to see more evidence of it than I do.

INTERVIEWER. The critics?

PINTER. It's a great mistake to pay any attention to *them.* I think, you see, that this is an age of such overblown publicity and overemphatic pinning down. I'm a very good example of a writer who can write, but I'm not as good as all that. I'm just a writer; and I think that I've been overblown tremendously because there's a dearth of really fine writing, and people tend to make too much of a meal. All you can do is try to write as well as you can.

INTERVIEWER. Do you think your plays will be performed fifty years from now? Is universality a quality you consciously strive for?

PINTER. I have no idea whether my plays will be performed in fifty years, and it's of no moment to me. I'm pleased when what I write makes sense in South America or Yugoslavia—it's gratifying. But I certainly don't strive for universality—I've got enough to strive for just writing a bloody play!

INTERVIEWER. Do you think the success you've known has changed your writing?

PINTER. No, but it did become more difficult. I think I've gone beyond something now. When I wrote the first three plays in 1957 I wrote them from the point of view of *writing* them; the whole world of putting on plays was quite remote—I knew they could never be done in the Reps I was acting in, and the West End and London were somewhere on the other side of the moon. So I wrote these plays completely unselfconsciously. There's no question that over the years it's become more difficult to preserve the kind of freedom that's essential to writing, but when I do write, it's there. For a while it became more difficult to avoid the searchlights and all that. And it took me five years to write a stage play, *The Homecoming,* after *The Caretaker.* I did a lot of things in the meantime, but writing a stage play, which is what I really wanted to do, I couldn't. Then I wrote *The Homecoming,* for good or bad, and I felt much better. But *now* I'm back in the same boat—I want to write a play, it buzzes all the time in me, and I can't put pen to paper. Something people don't realize is the great boredom one has with oneself, and just to see those words come down again on paper, I think oh Christ, everything I do seems to be predictable, unsatisfactory, and hopeless. It keeps me awake. Distractions don't matter to me—if I had something to write I would write it. Don't ask me why I want to keep on with plays at all!

INTERVIEWER. Do you think you'd ever use freer techniques as a way of starting writing again?

PINTER. I can enjoy them in other people's plays—I thought the *Marat/Sade* was a damn good evening, and other very different plays like *The Caucasian Chalk Circle* I've also enjoyed. But I'd never use such stage techniques myself.

INTERVIEWER. Does this make you feel behind the times in any way?

PINTER. I *am* a very traditional playwright—for instance I insist on having a curtain in all my plays. I write curtain lines for that reason! And even when directors like Peter Hall or Claude Régy in Paris want to do away with them, I insist they stay. For me everything has to do with shape, structure, and overall unity. All this jamboree in "Happenings" and eight-hour movies is great fun for the people concerned, I'm sure . . .

INTERVIEWER. Shouldn't they be having fun?

PINTER. If they're all having fun I'm delighted, but count me out completely, I wouldn't stay more than five minutes. The trouble is I find it all so *noisy,* and I like quiet things. There seems to be such a jazz and jaggedness in so much modern art, and a great deal of it is inferior to its models: Joyce contains so much of Burroughs, for example, in his experimental techniques, though Burroughs is a fine writer on his own. This doesn't mean I don't regard myself as a contemporary writer: I mean, I'm *here.*

Language and Silence

by Martin Esslin

That Pinter has added a new band of colours to the spectrum of English stage dialogue is attested by the frequent use of terms like "Pinteresque language" or "Pinterese" in current dramatic criticism. Some of the more obvious features of his use of language, such as recurrent tautological repetition, on the pattern "He's old. Not young. No, I wouldn't call him young. Not youthful, certainly. Elderly, I'd say. I'd call him old" have been copied to the point of self-parody by a large number of aspiring authors. And the bad imitations have inevitably cast a shadow over the original user and, indeed, discoverer of these linguistic absurdities, which had hitherto largely escaped the observant ears of playwrights. Yet these most easily recognisable features of Pinter's dialogue are, on the whole, the most superficial aspects of his artistry; even their function in the over-all picture has been largely misunderstood. While Pinter undoubtedly has an uncannily accurate ear for the linguistic solecisms of the English vernacular spoken by ordinary people, it is neither his special intention nor foremost dramatic purpose merely to amuse his audience by confronting them with accurately observed examples of linguistic nonsense and thus giving them the pleasure of *recognising* the linguistic mistakes of others and feeling superior to them. It may be true that a good deal of Pinter's initial success was due to this kind of audience reaction, and he may even, occasionally, have succumbed to the temptation of exploiting it. Yet if his work is seen as a whole it will be recognised that he has also resisted this temptation, and with considerable success, not only by discarding plays like *The Hothouse* (which might have been regarded as an overindulgence in Pinterese) but also by moving out of

"Language and Silence." From Martin Esslin, *The Peopled Wound* (New York: Doubleday & Company, Inc., 1970).

the sphere of low-life dialogue in the plays that followed the success of *The Caretaker* (*The Lover, The Collection,* and later *Tea Party* and *The Basement*); by avoiding the tricks of the more obvious Pinterese in a play that might well have given a great deal of opportunity for self-copying and self-parody—*The Homecoming*; and finally by abandoning naturalistic action and dialogue altogether in the next phase of his development—the highly compressed stage poetry of recollected experience in *Landscape* and *Silence.*

A true understanding of Pinter's use of language must, I believe, be based on deeper, more fundamental considerations. It must start from an examination of the function of language in stage dialogue generally—and indeed from considerations of the use of language in ordinary human intercourse itself. For here—at least as far as the English language is concerned—Pinter has given us added insight into—has, in a certain measure, even *discovered*—the fact that traditional stage dialogue has always greatly overestimated the degree of logic that governs the use of language, the amount of information that language is actually able to impart on the stage, as in life. People on the stage, from Sophocles to Shakespeare to Rattigan, have always spoken more clearly, more directly, more to the purpose than they would ever have done in real life. This is obvious enough in verse drama, which had to obey not only the rules of prosody but also those of the ancient art of rhetoric, which concerned itself with the ways in which speech could be made as clear, well proportioned, and easily assimilated as possible. So strong was this tradition that it even persisted in naturalistic drama, although it was sometimes superficially disguised: the finest speeches in Ibsen or Shaw are as brilliantly rhetorical as those of Cicero or Demosthenes. And even in the scenes of light conversation in the exposition of these plays, the main emphasis lies on the elegance with which the essential *information* about the antecedents of the plot, the motivation of the characters, is conveyed, broken up perhaps into seemingly casually arranged fragments, but nevertheless in a discursive, explicit style.

It was only gradually that a certain defectiveness of communication between characters—who talk past each other rather than to each other—was introduced by dramatists like Strindberg or Wedekind; and that "oblique" dialogue in which the text hints at a hidden subtext was brought in by Chekhov, as in the climactic scene of *The Cherry Orchard* discussed in an earlier chapter of this book, when the real action—Lopakhin's failure to declare himself to Varya—is taking place beneath a trivial exchange about a missing article of clothing. But this scene was elaborately *prepared* by Chekhov: he had taken care in the preceding scene to make it quite explicit to the audience that they were to expect Lopakhin's offer of marriage. Pinter's technique continues Chekhov's use of such "oblique" dialogue, but carries it much further.

A comparison between two climactic closing scenes by the two playwrights might serve to illustrate this point: In the closing scene of Chekhov's *Uncle Vanya,* the chief characters have lost their hope of love and fulfillment. Vanya turns to Sonia and expresses his feelings in a highly explicit outburst:

> My child, there's such a weight on my heart! Oh, if only you knew how my heart aches!

And Sonia replies:

> Well, what can we do? We must go on living! (*A pause.*) We shall go on living, Uncle Vanya. We shall live through a long, long succession of days and tedious evenings. We shall patiently suffer the trials which Fate imposes on us; we shall work for others, now and in our old age, and we shall have no rest. . . .

Having described the reality of their lives to come, Sonia turns to talk of their last remaining great hope of eternal rest—in death:

> We shall rest! We shall hear the angels, we shall see all the heavens covered with stars like diamonds, we shall see all earthly evil, all our sufferings swept away by the grace which will fill the whole world, and our life will become peaceful, gentle and sweet as a caress. I believe it, I believe it. . . . Poor, poor Uncle Vanya, you're crying. . . . You've had no joy in life, but wait, Uncle Vanya, wait . . . we shall rest . . . We shall rest. . . . We shall rest!

A magnificent piece of writing, but surely very far removed from the way in which a girl like Sonia would use language in a real situation of this kind. The rhetorical heritage is still very strong in Chekhov's style. There *is* an element of "obliqueness" present even here, however, for while Sonia professes to *believe* in the joys of eternal bliss in heaven, we know that what she is saying is *not* what she really believes; she is using the picture of heavently bliss as a last despairing attempt at bringing consolation to Uncle Vanya. It is in the contrast between what is being said and what lies behind it that the poignancy and also the innovatory modernity of Chekhov's approach to language in drama appears.

Pinter, in the final scene of *The Birthday Party,* which portrays a situation that is analogous to the close of *Uncle Vanya*—the loss of the hope of love suffered by Meg—goes infinitely further than Chekhov. Pinter's characters do not talk explicitly about the situation at all. Meg knows, deep down, that Stanley has gone, but she cannot and will not admit it to herself; and Petey is too inarticulate to offer a speech of consolation like Sonia's:

> *Meg.* I was the belle of the ball.
> *Petey.* Were you?
> *Meg.* Oh yes. They all said I was.
> *Petey.* I bet you were too.
> *Meg.* Oh, it's true. I was.
> (*Pause.*)
> I know I was.

Four times Meg repeats that she was the belle of the ball—the disastrous party through which her substitute son was destroyed and taken away from her. It is quite clear that she does not in fact want to say anything about the impression she actually made at that party. She is merely trying to hang on to the illusion that everything is still as it was, that the disastrous party was not a disaster but the success she had hoped for. The fourfold *repetition* of the statement does not derive from any desire to say the same thing four times; it is no more than a sign of the desperateness of her attempt, her pitiful determination not to let the realisation of the disaster dawn on her. Hence the repetition of the statement is more relevant than the statement, and the explicit, "discursive" content of the statement itself. Similarly Petey's affirmation that the statement is true merely expresses his compassion, his despair, and, above all, his inability to do anything towards making Meg acknowledge or realise the true position. The dramatic effect of this brilliantly moving, brilliantly economical and concise passage of dialogue is entirely due to the complete contradiction between the words that are spoken and the emotional and psychological *action* that underlies them. Here the language has almost totally lost its rhetorical, informative element and has fully merged into dramatic action.

It is true that in a passage of dialogue like this there is little verbal communication between the characters, in that neither Meg nor Petey informs the other of any fact she or he wants him or her to know. Yet to sum up this state of affairs by labelling such a passage a "dialogue of non-communication" completely misses the point. Pinter is far from wanting to say that language is incapable of establishing true communication between human beings; he merely draws our attention to the fact that in life human beings rarely make use of language for that purpose, at least so far as spoken language is concerned. People interact not so much logically as emotionally through language; and their tone of voice, the emotional colour of the words, is often far more significant than their exact meanings by their dictionary definition. We all know that an outburst of name-calling by one person against another is basically an act of aggression, an assault by verbal blows in which the violence of the emotion behind the words is far more important than their content. Where animals use physical action and physical contact (such as sniffing each other, catching each other's fleas), human beings, through the power of speech, can substitute verbal contact and verbal action (small talk about the weather, exchange of information about one's minor ailments, abuse or words of endearment). What matters in most oral verbal contact is therefore more what people are *doing* to each other through it than the conceptual content of what they are saying.

In drama, dialogue is ultimately a form of *action;* it is the element of action, the interaction between the characters, their reactions to each other, that constitutes the truly *dramatic* element in stage dialogue, its essential aspect in the context of drama, apart from, and over and above, all the other values embodied in the writing: its wit, lucidity, elegance of structure and logical development, depth of thought, persuasiveness, rhythm, imagery, mellifluousness, and sheer beauty as poetry—all the rhetorical and literary qualities that *could also* be appreciated *outside* the context of drama.

Being essentially action, dramatic dialogue is not necessarily the dominant element in the playwright's armoury: it may be equally important as, or even less so than the nonverbal actions of the characters and, indeed, their silences. Traditionally, however, because of the origins of dramatic writing in the art of oratory, dialogue has been the dominant element in drama. Hence the tendency for drama to involve highly articulate characters, the only ones who would naturally interact in terms of brilliantly phrased speech. This showed itself in the need to *stylise* verbal expression by the use of verse, which relieved the playwright of the need to imitate the real speech of characters who in reality would have been inarticulate, or at least far from possessing the powers of expression with which they seemed to be endowed on the stage; or, in later naturalistic drama, the tendency to place the action among people who would be highly articulate in real life: the elegant wits of Wilde, the eloquent intellectuals of Shaw. Only when it was recognised that the verbal element need not be the dominant aspect of drama, or at least that it was not the content of what was said that mattered most but the action that it embodied, and that inarticulate, incoherent, tautological, and nonsensical speech might be as dramatic as verbal brilliance when it was treated simply as an element of action, only then did it become possible to place inarticulate characters in the centre of the play and make their unspoken emotions transparent. Pinter is among the discoverers of this highly significant aspect of drama.

If we examine some of Pinter's favourite linguistic and stylistic devices in the light of these considerations, we shall find that, far from being mere verbal absurdities held up to ridicule, they do in fact illuminate the mental processes that lie behind the ill-chosen or nonsensical words; and that in each case superficially similar quirks of language may serve quite different dramatic functions.

Take the most obvious of these, the one most frequently attributed to Pinter as a mere mannerism: repetition. Each time Pinter's characters repeat themselves, or each other's phrases, the playwright employs the device of repetition to fulfill a definite function in the action; if, for example, at the beginning of *The Birthday Party* Meg, having served Petey his corn flakes, asks:

Meg. Are they nice?
Petey. Very nice.
Meg. I thought they'd be nice.

the emptiness of the dialogue clearly indicates the emptiness of the characters' relationship with each other, the boredom of their lives and yet their determination to go on making friendly conversation. So this short dialogue of no more than ten words, three of which are repetitious of "nice," which on the surface conveys no worthwhile *conceptual* information whatever, does in fact compress a very considerable amount of dramatic *information*—this being the exposition of the play—and dramatic *action,* i.e. the vain attempt at conversation, the desire to be friendly, into an astonishingly brief space.

If, on the other hand, Davies in *The Caretaker,* talking about his ex-wife's slovenliness, mentions the saucepan in which he found some of her underclothing, repeats himself, saying: "The pan for vegetables, it was. The vegetable pan . . ." the repetition serves a completely different purpose: it shows us this inarticulate man's struggle to find the correct word, the *mot juste.* Traditional stage dialogue tended to err on the side of assuming that people have the right expression always ready to suit the occasion. In Pinter's dialogue we can watch the desperate struggles of his characters to find the correct expression; we are thus enabled to observe them in the—very dramatic—act of struggling for communication, sometimes succeeding, often failing. And when they have got hold of a formulation, they hold on to it, savour it, and repeat it to enjoy their achievement, like Gus in *The Dumb Waiter,* when he recalls the time they killed a girl:

> . . . It was a mess though, wasn't it? What a mess. Honest I can't remember a mess like that one. They don't seem to hold together like men, women. A looser texture, like. Didn't she spread, eh? She didn't half spread. Kaw!

The pleasure with which Gus dwells on the word *mess* and *spread* is evident: not because he enjoyed killing the girl, quite the contrary, but because, being an inarticulate person who has trouble finding the expressive phrase, he loves to play with and savour it once he has got hold of it, and does not want to let it go. He is delighted to have found the expressive image of the girl's body dissolving like butter: "she spread." So while, on one level, he is worried and unhappy about his job as a killer and deplores having had to liquidate that girl, on another he revels in the happy feeling of having expressed his thought well. This is another example of how dialogue that is primitive and crude when judged by the standards of rhetoric can be astonishingly subtle, ironic, and psychologically penetrating if considered as an expression of character in action—drama.

As against the use of repetition to show a character's *enjoyment* at having found the *mot juste,* there is repetition as a form of hysterical irritation: for example, so obsessed is McCann in *The Birthday Party* with the unpleasantness of what he and Goldberg will have to do to Stanley that he breaks out:

> Let's finish and go. Let's get it over and go. Get the thing done. Let's finish the bloody thing. Let's get the thing done and go!

McCann's hysteria emerges not only from the frantic rhythm with which these sentences are phrased but also from the obsessive permutation of the same elements—"finish," "go," "get done."

Conversely, Pinter uses repetition to show how a character gradually learns to accept a fact that at first he had difficulty taking in. Having been terrorised by Mick, Davies in *The Caretaker* asks Aston:

> *Davies.* Who was that feller?
> *Aston.* He's my brother.
> *Davies.* Is he? He's a bit of a joker, en' he?
> *Aston.* Uh.
> *Davies.* Yes . . . he's a real joker.
> *Aston.* He's got a sense of humour.
> *Davies.* Yes, I noticed.
> (*Pause.*)
> He's a real joker, that lad, you can see that.
> (*Pause.*)
> *Aston.* Yes, he tends . . . he tends to see the funny side of things.
> *Davies.* Well, he's got a sense of humour, en' he?
> *Aston.* Yes.
> *Davies.* Yes, you could tell that.
> (*Pause.*)

Here the manner in which Davies takes up Aston's phrase about the "sense of humour" and the way in which he punctuates his realisation of Mick's character with "I noticed," "you can see that," and "you could tell that" allows the audience to witness the slow sinking in of the facts, the gradual evaluation of the man he met, his eventual and increasingly bitter coming to terms with these facts. Two repeated phrases are interlocked in this passage ("He's a joker/got a sense of humour" and "I noticed/can see/can tell that") and again their various permutations in the mouth of first the one and then the other character give the dialogue a definite poetic shape, a musical form of theme and variations, of strophe and antistrophe: psychological realism and a poet's control over the formal element in language are here fused in a way highly characteristic of Pinter.

Repetition, which, as Pinter has discovered, is an aspect of real speech that stage dialogue had neglected under the influence of the rhetorical tradition (which rejects recurrence of the same word as stylistically inelegant), is, of course, also one of the most important elements of poetry—particularly in the form of whole phrases that recur as refrains, for example in ballad metre—on the realistic level. Pinter uses the refrain-like recurrence of whole sentences to show that people in real life do not deliver well-thought-out set speechs but tend to mix various logical strands of thought, which intermingle without any apparent connection; while the structure of rhetorical or written language tends to be logical, that of spoken language is associative. In the first act of *The Caretaker,* Aston tells Davies that there is a family of Indians living in the house next door. Davies immediately reacts:

Davies. Blacks?
Aston. I don't see much of them.
Davies. Blacks, eh?

The conversation then turns to other matters, and Davies embarks on his story about his odyssey to the monastery at Luton, where he had been told the monks handed out shoes to the poor. Having reached the climax of that story, he is about to introduce the punch line:

. . . You know what that bastard monk said to me?
(*Pause.*)
How many more Blacks you got around here then?
Aston. What?
Davies. You got any more Blacks around here?

Without any *logical* motivation the question about the Blacks re-emerges a minute or more after it was first mooted. But the association is clear enough: the hatred and indignation Davies feels for the monk who treated him so badly has reawakened the emotion of fear and hatred against that other arch-enemy of his—the coloured community.

Similarly, in Davies' long speech of hatred against Aston, when he believes that Mick will support him in giving him control of the house and he tries to assert his superiority over Aston as a former inmate of a mental institution, we find several lines of thought mixed to give a refrain-like effect:

> . . . I'm a sane man! So don't start mucking me about. I'll be all right as long as you keep your place. Just you keep your place, that's all. *Because I can tell you, your brother's got his eye on you.* He knows all about you. I got a friend there, don't worry about that. I got a true pal there! Treating me like dirt! Why'd you invite me in here in the first place if you was going to treat me like this? You think you're better than me you got another think coming. I know enough. They had you inside one of them places before, they can have you inside again. *Your brother's got his eye on you!* They can put the pincers on your head again, man. . . . [My italics.]

It is clear that this type of associative structure, in which several basic thoughts (I am better than you because I am sane, you have been in a mental institution—your brother is my friend, he has his eye on you) intermingle in ever-recurring variations belongs on the whole to characters of Davies' primitive mentality. But Pinter also uses it, in an appropriately modified form, in the mouth of one of his most sophisticated characters, Harry, the rich clothing manufacturer in *The Collection:*

> Bill's a slum boy, you see, he's got a slum sense of humour. That's why I never take him along to parties. Because he's got a slum mind. I have nothing against slum minds *per se,* you understand, nothing at all. There's a certain kind of slum mind which is perfectly all right in a slum, but when this kind of slum mind get out of the slum it sometimes persists, you see, it rots everything. That's what Bill is. There's something faintly putrid about him, don't you find? Like a slug. There's nothing wrong with slugs in their place, but he's a slum slug; there's nothing wrong with slum slugs in their place, but this one won't keep his place—he crawls all over the walls of nice houses, leaving slime, don't you, boy? He confirms stupid sordid little stories just to amuse himself, while everyone else has to run round in circles to get to the root of the matter and smooth the whole thing out. All he

can do is sit and suck his bloody hand and decompose like the filthy putrid slum slug he is. . . .

Here the structure is apparently one of rigid logic, even of syllogism, but only apparently. The real motivation for the erection of this structure of pseudo-logic is to give an opportunity to hammer away at the humiliating terms *slum* and *slug;* the repetition indicates the degree of Harry's obsession with Bill and his hatred of him, it is also deliberately used by him as a means of aggression, of mental torture and humiliation towards Bill. And again the refrain-like recurrence of the same type of phrase ("I have nothing against," "There is nothing wrong") gives this highly realistic and closely observed reproduction of genuine speech patterns a musical-poetic structure.

In Harry's diatribe the emotional charge of jealousy, hatred, and contempt underlies the associative structure of his speech. In other instances it is the absence of emotion, the determination to avoid saying what ought to be said, that leads to associative and equally repetitious sequences of words. When Davies, in *The Caretaker,* first encounters Mick, is frightened by him and asks who he is, Mick, who wants to torment him by keeping him on tenterhooks, embarks on a long diatribe, which is quite obviously intended to convey no information whatever:

> You know, believe it or not, you've got a funny kind of resemblance to a bloke I once knew in Shoreditch. Actually he lived in Aldgate. I was staying with a cousin in Camden Town. This chap, he used to have a pitch in Finsbury Park, just by the bus depot. When I got to know him I found out he was brought up in Putney. That didn't make any difference to me. I know quite a few people who were born in Putney. Even if they weren't born in Putney, they were born in Fulham. The only trouble was, he wasn't born in Putney, he was only brought up in Putney. It turned out he was born in the Caledonian Road, just before you get to the Nag's Head.

Not only is this passage, in its total nonsensicality, highly comic, not only does it prolong Davies' and the audience's suspense, it also shows the thought process that prompts Mick: one London place name simply leads him on to the next. We can clearly follow his method in making up a long and meaningless speech, which ironically apes the exchanges of reminiscences between new acquaintances who want to break the ice between themselves by recalling mutual friends with a maximum of circumstantial detail. So transparent is the associative mechanism here that we are also fully aware that Mick is malevolently enjoying himself at Davies' expense.

It is by an analogous use of associative linguistic structure that Pinter indicates that a character is lying. Here, too, the story is being made up as it goes along, and often merely from the *sound* of the words, as in Solto's reply to the question how he got to Australia, in *Night School:*

> *Solto.* By sea. How do you think? I worked my passage. And what a trip. I was only a pubescent. I killed a man with my own hands, a six-foot-ten Lascar from Madagascar.
> *Annie.* From Madagascar?
> *Solto.* Sure. A Lascar.
> *Milly.* Alaska?
> *Solto.* Madagascar.
> (*Pause.*)
> *Walter.* It's happened before.
> *Solto.* And it'll happen again.

It is quite clear that Solto thought of Madagascar only because the term Lascar suggested it. Walter's interjection, that it happened before, indicates that he is fully aware of the spuriousness of the story and the intention behind it; namely, the braggart's desire to impress. Hence by his remark he shows himself unimpressed, while Solto, by insisting that it happened and will happen again, feebly insists on his veracity, but without carrying any conviction.

The braggart is a stock figure of comedy and has been from time immemorial, and so, of course, have been the braggart's stories and lies. Here Pinter is therefore moving along very traditional lines; where his special talent shines through is in his ability to make the often very pathetic thought-processes behind the tall stories utterly transparent to the audience: these liars are carried along, almost passively, by the limited range of their imaginations, the paucity of possible associations that can lead them on from one word to the next. When Walter, again in *Night School,* brags to Sally about his success as a prison librarian, for example, he is, very much against his will and better judgement, driven into a mention of rare manuscripts:

. . . Well, funny enough, I've had a good bit to do with rare manuscripts in my time. I used to know a bloke who ran a business digging them up. . . . Rare manuscripts. Out of tombs. I used to give him a helping hand when I was on the loose. Very well paid it was, too. You see, they were nearly always attached to a corpse, these manuscripts, you had to lift up the pelvis bone with a pair of tweezers. Big tweezers. Can't leave fingerprints on a corpse, you see. Canon law. . . .

(The germ of this speech is already contained in Pinter's early novel *The Dwarfs,* where Pete tries to impress a girl during a party. In the passage in *Night School,* however, the idea has been considerably and brilliantly developed and expanded.) It is only superficially that a speech like this one is funny. On a deeper level, it reveals an underprivileged individual's desperate attempt to impress the girl, the mixture of ignorance and half-baked information with which his mind is stocked, the vagueness of his ideas. Rare manuscripts to him suggest archaeology, and archaeology, tombs. Somehow he has to invent for himself a way in which these two vague ideas can be related, hence the suggestion that rare manuscripts are found in tombs. Hence the association with skeletons; hence, again, the urge to mention one of the few technical terms from anatomy he knows—"pelvis"—which leads to the association with the cliché of the soap opera involving an operation: it is here that tweezers are always mentioned. And this brings the ex-convict Walter back to his own sphere: to explain the tweezers he gets back to his own world, that of the petty thief who does not want to leave fingerprints. To retrieve this lapse he has to take covering action by mentioning canon law. While it is unlikely that the audience will be wholly conscious of the exact way in which such a chain of associations is built up, they can certainly follow the main line of the underlying thought-process and thus partake in the *action* that this speech portrays, Walter's desperate attempt, on the one hand, to establish his intellectual and social superiority and his equally desperate efforts, on the other, to extricate himself from the more and more difficult traps and pitfalls he creates for himself.

Always, in Pinter's world, personal inadequacy expresses itself in an inadequacy to cope with and to use language. The inability to communicate, and to *communicate in the correct terms,* is felt by the characters as a mark of inferiority; that is why they tend to dwell upon and to stress the hard or unusual "educated" words they know.

Solto, in the rodomontade quoted above, casually introduces the unusual, and to him no doubt highly refined, term "pubescent," Walter talks about "canon law," "pelvis," "rare manuscripts"; Mick in *The Caretaker,* on his first confrontation with Davies, speaks of someone the tramp reminds him of, who had a *penchant* for nuts:

> Had a penchant for nuts. That's what it was. Nothing else but a penchant. Couldn't eat enough of them. Peanuts, walnuts, brazil nuts, monkey nuts, wouldn't touch a piece of fruitcake.

Note, again, the laying bare of the mechanism of the lie: the false circumstantial detail contained in the associative use of the names of different kinds of nuts. The introduction of the "refined" term *penchant,* however, serves to emphasise Mick's claim to superior education, intelligence, and *savoir-faire.* It is thus equivalent to an *act of aggression.* Again and again veritable duels of this type develop among Pinter's characters. The memorable dispute about whether one says "light the kettle" or "light the gas" in *The Dumb Waiter* belongs in this category. Words like "penchant" and "pubescent" are proofs of superior general education. The use of technical terms and professional jargon, on the other hand, establishes the speaker's superiority in his own chosen field and gives him the advantages of belonging to a freemasonry, an inner circle of people who are able to exclude intruders and interlopers. The use of technical jargon thus corresponds to the enclosed rooms and protected spaces that Pinter's characters tend to covet and to defend against outsiders. When Mick finally turns against Davies and initiates the move that will expel him from the home he has been seeking, he overwhelms him with a demonstration of his ignorance of the skills he alleges Davies claimed when applying for the post of a caretaker in his house:

> *Mick.* . . . I only told you because I understood you were an experienced first-class professional interior and exterior decorator.
>
> *Davies.* Now look here—
>
> *Mick.* You mean you wouldn't know how to fit teal-blue, copper and parchement linoleum squares and have those colours re-echoed in the walls?
>
> *Davies.* Now, look here, where'd you get—?
>
> *Mick.* You wouldn't be able to decorate out a table in afromosia teak veneer, an armchair in oatmeal tweed and a beech frame settee with a woven sea-grass seat?

Davies. I never said that!
Mick. Christ! I must have been under a false impression!
Davies. I never said it!
Mick. You're a bloody impostor, mate!

Davies' inability to comprehend the technical jargon of the interior decorator seals what, in effect, is his death sentence. In fact he had never directly claimed any such knowledge, but had merely tacitly nodded his approval when Mick, using the selfsame terms, had tempted him with the job of caretaker while outlining his grandiose plans for converting the derelict dwelling into a "penthouse." Incomprehension and the inability to express himself is clearly stated to be the reason for his loss of favour with Mick:

> Honest. I can take nothing you say at face value. Every word you speak is open to any number of different interpretations. Most of what you say is lies. You're violent, you're erratic, you're just completely unpredictable. You're nothing else but a wild animal, when you come down to it. You're a barbarian. . . .

The ability to communicate is here equated with civilisation, even the possession of a claim to being human. The loser in a contest about words and their meaning loses his claim to live. Power, the power over life or death, derives from the ability to make one's opponent accept the meaning of words chosen by the dominant partner. When Davies, earlier in the play, ventures to remark that Aston, Mick's brother, is "a bit of a funny bloke," Mick stares at him in indignant amazement:

Mick. Funny? Why?
Davies. Well . . . he's funny . . .
Mick. What's funny about him?
(*Pause.*)
Davies. Not liking work.
Mick. What's funny about that?
Davies. Nothing.
(*Pause.*)
Mick. I don't call it funny.
Davies. Nor me.

His surrender is both abject and complete. A disagreement about the meaning of a term has become a fundamental, existential contest of wills. Words are thus of vital importance. And yet, it is not so much the words themselves as the existential situations they conceal and reveal. It is no coincidence that the climactic turning point of *The Homecoming* arises from a "philosophical" discussion, Lenny's attempt to draw his brother Teddy into an argument about being and nonbeing, words and the realities behind them:

Lenny. Well, for instance, take a table. Philosophically speaking. What is it?

Teddy. A table.

Lenny. Ah. You mean it's nothing else but a table. Well, some people would envy your certainty, wouldn't they, Joey? For instance, I've got a couple of friends of mine, we often sit round the Ritz Bar having a few liqueurs, and they are always saying things like that, you know, things like: Take a table, take it. All right, I say, *take* it, *take* a table, but once you've taken it, what you going to do with it? Once you've got hold of it, where you going to take it?

Max. You'd probably sell it.

Lenny. You wouldn't get much for it.

Joey. Chop it up for firewood.

(*Lenny looks at him and laughs.*)

Ruth. Don't be too sure though. You've forgotten something. Look at me. I . . . move my leg. That's all it is. But I wear . . . underwear . . . which moves with me . . . it . . . captures your attention. Perhaps you misinterpret. The action is simple. It's a leg . . . moving. My lips move. Why don't you restrict . . . your observations to that? Perhaps the fact that they move is more significant . . . than the words which come through them. You must bear that . . . possibility . . . in mind.

Perhaps the fact that the lips move is more significant than the words that come through them! This key sentence not only touches the basis of Pinter's practice of the use of dramatic dialogue, it also reveals his fundamental philosophical attitude, his search, through and in spite of an obsessive preoccupation with language, its nuances, its meaning, its beauty, for the area of reality that lies *behind* the use of language. It is not the word "table" that matters, but the way you *take* the table, how you *act* on it and how it *acts* on you, what it does to you. The lips that move are more significant, ultimately, than the words that come through them, the leg and the underwear that moves with it have more reality, because they are an action that creates an immediate response, than any of the polite words that a respectable professor's wife like Ruth might utter. Or, to put it differently, it matters little whether Mick's or Davies' interpretation of the word "funny" is the correct one; what is essential and existentially important is that Mick makes Davies accept *his* definition of the word's meaning.

Again and again in Pinter's plays, language becomes the medium through which a contest of wills is fought out, sometimes overtly, as in the disputes about the correct expression to be used or about the correct meaning of a given word or phrase, sometimes beneath the surface of the explicit subject matter of the dialogue. The brainwashing of Stanley by Goldberg and McCann in *The Birthday Party* shows the transition from the one mode to the other with particular clarity. It opens with specific questions referring to Stanley's real situation:

> Why do you behave so badly, Webber? Why do you force that old man out to play chess?

Yet gradually the questions become more and more fantastic, more and more abstract, until in the end we are indeed made aware that it is the lips that are moving, and the rage with which they move, that matter, rather than the words they utter. Nevertheless the words are of the utmost importance; not through their surface meaning, but through the colour and texture of their sound *and* their *associations* of meaning. At first Goldberg and McCann bombard Stanley with questions about specific crimes, which, however, are so contradictory that it is clear that he could not really have committed all of them. At one point he is asked: "Why did you kill your wife?" A few lines later his crime is: "Why did you never get married?"

As the cross-examination proceeds, it becomes ever more obvious that it is an expression of Stanley's *general* feelings of guilt, of his tormentors' general conviction that he deserves punishment. The long list of venial and mortal sins, major and minor transgressions, which is unleashed upon poor Stanley—"You stuff yourself with dry toast. You contaminate womankind. Why don't you pay the rent? Why do you pick your nose? What about Ireland?"—covers the whole gamut of possible sources of guilt feelings, from embarrassment over social gaffes (picking one's nose), collective national guilt feelings about crimes committed by one's country (in Ireland for the Englishman Stanley Webber), minor lapses (such as eating too much toast), to the major sins of lechery and, worst of all, cheating at the national sport: "Who watered the wicket in Melbourne?" (which so baffled the first translator of the play into German that he rendered it by a sentence which, translated back, reads: "Who urinated against the city gate of Melbourne?") until it culminates in the final, existential question of why the chicken crossed the road, and which came first, the chicken or the egg—in other words why Stanley has the effrontery to exist, to be alive at all. The proliferation of images, grotesquely juxtaposed and subtly intensified, establishes this long scene as a kind of poem, a structure of images which constitutes a set of variations on a basic theme. The chief character of the play is thrown, as it were, into a whirlpool of language, which batters him into insensitivity.

Ten years after Pinter wrote *The Birthday Party,* Peter Handke, a young protagonist of the theatrical avant-garde in Germany, achieved considerable success with a new kind of dramatic spectacle, which he called *Sprechstücke* (word plays); these consist of long structures of pure language uttered by speakers who do not represent any specific characters. By confronting the audience with permutations of words and associations on a given theme (the future; cries for help; insults; or the sources of guilt feelings) these set up linguistic fields of force, from which each member of the audience must, willynilly, assemble his own personal experience of hope, helplessness, rage, or guilt. Pinter not only anticipated this "new" experimental form, but also demonstrated how it could be integrated and made to work within a more traditional framework of drama.

Brilliant as the brainwashing scene in *The Birthday Party* is, Pinter's use of language became far subtler in his later plays. When Lenny first meets Ruth in *The Homecoming,* he tells her two long, and seemingly gratuitous, stories. As in *The Birthday Party*'s brainwashing scene, these are linguistic structures designed to evoke feelings of guilt and terror in the listener; but they are far more subtly orchestrated, far less obviously abstract *tours de force.* Having just met Ruth late at night and alone in his house, Lenny at first engages her in the usual small talk. Then suddenly, out of a speech about her visit to Venice and his feeling that he might have seen Venice had he served in the last war, he confronts her with a clearly erotic proposition:

Lenny. . . . Do you mind if I hold your hand?
Ruth. Why?
Lenny. Just a touch.
(*He stands and goes to her.*)
Just a tickle.
Ruth. Why?
(*He looks down at her.*)
Lenny. I'll tell you why.
(*Slight pause.*)

Lenny then launches into his first long story, which seems totally unrelated to the question he promised to answer; namely, why he wants to touch Ruth. The story starts on a formal linguistic level, almost like the opening sentences of a novel:

> One night, not too long ago, one night down by the docks, I was standing alone under an arch, watching all the men jibbing the boom, out in the harbour, and playing about with the yardarm—

Note the use of technical terms of nautical language as an indication of expertise, of being an insider. Ruth and the audience will now expect to hear that Lenny (whose occupation is a mystery) might turn out to have something to do with the sea. But at this point the story—and the language—suddenly change gear: "—when a certain lady came up to me and made me a certain proposal."

Now we are in terminology of the British popular press when it deals, as politely and respectably as is possible under the circumstances, with sexual matters, and above all sex crimes:

> This lady had been searching for me for days. She'd lost track of my whereabouts. However, the fact was she eventually caught up with me, and when she caught up with me she made me this certain proposal. Well, this proposal wasn't entirely out of order and normally I would have subscribed to it. I mean I would have subscribed to it in the normal course of events. The only trouble was—

and here the language again enters, abruptly, another sphere altogether:

> —The only trouble was she was falling apart with the pox.

This is another field of technical jargon: the professional talk of pimps and prostitutes. Lenny has shown his hand; he has indicated that this is his world. What is more, he goes on to discuss, very dispassionately and coolly, his desire to kill the girl there and then:

> . . . and the fact is, that as killings go, it would have been a simple matter, nothing to it.

and concludes the story with his decision *not* to kill her:

> But . . . in the end I thought . . . Aaah, why go to all the bother . . . you know, getting rid of the corpse and all that, getting yourself into a state of tension. So I just gave her another belt in the nose and a couple of turns of the boot and sort of left it at that.

Again it is the switching from the polite language of the newspaper crime report to the brutal vernacular of the criminal himself that makes the point. In answer to Ruth's question why he made her an erotic proposal Lenny has told her that being engaged in the business of prostitution, and being in a position to reject such proposals from other girls, he feels himself entitled to make such claims, and that, indeed, such claims should be regarded as an honour by the women to whom they are addressed. Ruth's reaction shows that she has understood the import of the story only too well. Displaying no surprise whatever, she instinctively or deliberately falls into the same technical jargon:

> *Ruth.* How did you know she was diseased?
> *Lenny.* How did I know?
> (*Pause.*)
> I decided she was.
> (*Silence.*)
> You and my brother are newly-weds, are you?

Having, by her lack of surprise and the technical language of her question, revealed that she comes from the same world, Ruth is, in Lenny's answer, sharply reminded by him that his power over his girls is absolute. If he decides that a girl is diseased, then she is diseased. The point is made. Lenny can change the subject and return to polite small talk. But it is merely a short break in the contest of wills. Again, to establish his determination to be brutal to women, be they helpless and old, Lenny tells his second long story about the lady who asked him to move her mangle while he was employed to clear the snow in the streets on a winter morning, but failed to give him a helping hand with the heavy object:

> So after a few minutes I said to her, now look here, why don't you stuff this iron mangle up your arse? Anyway, I said, they're out of date, you want to get a spin-drier. I had a good mind to give her a workover there and then, but as I was feeling jubilant with the snow-clearing I just gave her a short-arm jab to the belly and jumped on a bus outside. Excuse me, shall I take this ashtray out of your way?

The narration of a brutal assault on an old woman is directly linked to the seemingly trivial question about the ashtray. But in fact the ashtray and the glass that stands beside it become the focus for the first direct confrontation between Ruth and Lenny. She does not want to move the ashtray, and she wants to keep the glass, as she is still thirsty. And having been told of Lenny's capacity to be brutal to women and having taken it all in, Ruth openly challenges him: "If you take the glass . . . I'll take you." And she goes over to the attack:

(*She picks up the glass and lifts it towards him.*)
Ruth. Have a sip. Go on. Have a sip from my glass.
(*He is still.*)
Sit on my lap. Take a long cool sip.
(*She pats her lap. Pause.*)
(*She stands, moves to him with the glass.*)
Put your head back and open your mouth.
Lenny. Take that glass away from me.
Ruth. Lie on the floor. Go on. I'll pour it down your throat.
Lenny. What are you doing, making me some kind of proposal?
(*She laughs shortly, drains the glass.*)

Ruth has turned the tables completely. She has become the girl who makes a proposal to Lenny; but Lenny fails to do to her what he had boasted he had done to the girl who had made him that proposal.

The audience, witnessing the play for the first time, will of course not be consciously aware of *all* the information the playwright has subtly supplied in the shifts of linguistic levels, the echoing and re-echoing of key words (e.g. "proposal"). To them the strange night scene with its long and seemingly pointless narrative passages and the sudden contest of wills must seem "enigmatic," provocatively suggestive but barely penetrable. Dramatically this is an advantage, because it generates one of the most important elements in all drama —suspense. Yet, as in the best detective fiction, the clues are all provided, and with scrupulous fairness. They are present in the language itself, which lets us see through it into the depths of the unspoken thoughts and emotions of the two characters: Lenny propositions Ruth because he has sensed that she is like the girls with whom he deals in his profession. When she asks *why* he has propositioned her, he tells her, by gradually falling into the brutal trade language of the pimp, what he is and—by implication—what he thinks she may well be. And by her reaction—or rather the absence of a shocked reaction, the acceptance of a man who uses that kind of language as a matter of course—she clearly indicates that she does in fact belong to that same world. Hence Ruth's acceptance of the role of a prostitute when it is offered to her towards the end of the play, which tends to shock audiences so deeply, has already been anticipated in this scene of her first confrontation with Lenny. And so has the sovereign, disdainfully businesslike attitude with which she settles the terms of her new life by driving an exceedingly hard bargain; for in that first contest of wills she has shown herself fully Lenny's equal in ruthlessness.

In fact, if one analyses Pinter's work closely, one will find that behind the apparently random rendering of the colloquial vernacular there lies a rigorous economy of means; each word is essential to the total structure and decisively contributes to the ultimate, over-all effect aimed at. In this respect also, Pinter's use of language is that of a poet; there are no redundant words in true poetry, no empty patches, no mere fill-ins. Pinter's dramatic writing has the density of texture of true poetry.

That is why—as in poetry, the caesura; as in music, the pause—silences play such a large and essential part in Pinter's dialogue. Pinter uses two different terms for the punctuation of his dialogue by passages without speech: "Pause" and "Silence." In the above example, which has been analysed in some detail, when, at the end of Lenny's first narration, Ruth asks how he knew the girl in question was diseased (and thus reveals her lack of surprise and her familiarity with the vocabulary), Lenny's reaction is:

How did I know?
(*Pause.*)
I decided she was.
(*Silence.*)
You and my brother are newly-weds, are you?

The repetition of the question "How did I know?" shows Lenny's surprise at Ruth's reaction; he can hardly, as yet, believe that she would react in so matter-of-fact a way. The pause bridges the time he needs to take in the whole import of that reaction and to think out his reply. The silence after his reply and before he changes the subject indicates the much deeper caesura of the end of that section of the conversation. When Pinter asks for a *pause,* therefore, he indicates that intense thought processes are continuing, that unspoken tensions are mounting, whereas *silences* are notations for the end of a movement, the beginning of another, as between the movements of a symphony.

The pauses and silences in Pinter's play are the answer to Len's question in the novel *The Dwarfs,* when he was speaking about those poets who climb from word to word like stepping stones: "What do they do when they come to a line with no words in it at all?" The answer to that question is that *drama* is a kind of poetry that *can* find room for the emotional charge of the unspoken line. What speaks on the stage is the situation itself: the characters who confront each other in silence; what has gone before and the expectation, the suspense as to what will happen next. Pinter's pauses and silences are often the climaxes of his plays, the still centres of the storm, the nuclei of tension around which the whole action is structured: there is the "long silence" at the end of *The Caretaker,* when Davies' pleading for permission to remain in Aston's room elicits no answer. This "long silence" is the death of hope for the old man, Aston's refusal to forgive him, his expulsion from the warmth of a home—death. But as the curtain falls before he is seen to leave, it may also be the long silence before that final word of forgiveness is pronounced: the "line with no words in it" thus has all the ambiguity and complexity of true poetry, and it is also a metaphor, an image of overwhelming power.

At the close of *The Collection,* after Bill's "final" confession, his last version of the incident with James' wife, Stella—namely, that nothing happened between them at all—Pinter calls for a "long silence," after which James leaves the house. And then the silence continues as Harry and Bill remain sitting, facing each other. That silence contains an image of the despair and horror of their mutual dependence, above all of Bill's final failure to free himself from

Harry's domination. As the light fades on that image, James is seen returning to his own home and confronting his wife:

James. You didn't do anything, did you?
(*Pause.*)
He wasn't in your room. You just talked about it, in the lounge.
(*Pause.*)
That's the truth, isn't it?
(*Pause.*)
You just sat and talked about what you would do if you went to your room. That's what you did.
(*Pause.*)
Didn't you?
(*Pause.*)
That's the truth . . . isn't it?
(*Stella looks at him, neither confirming nor denying. Her face is friendly, sympathetic.*)

Stella's silence, her refusal to confirm or deny the story, is, in the true dramatic sense, an *action,* the pause that echoes each of James' questions *is a line of dialogue;* it is also a poetic image of one human being's mystery and impenetrability for another. Neither of these, it must again be stressed, has anything to do with man's *inability* to communicate with his fellow man; what is being demonstrated is man's—or in this case woman's—*unwillingness* to communicate, and indeed her partner's inability ever to be certain that, whether she speaks or remains silent, he can get hold of the real, the inner, personal truth of the matter.

The silence that is a *refusal* to communicate is one of the dominant images of Pinter's plays, from Bert's nonresponsiveness to Rose in his first play, *The Room,* to Beth's inability or unwillingness to hear, and to respond to, what Duff tells her in *Landscape.*

There is another speechlessness, however, in Pinter's work, the speechlessness of annihilation, of total collapse: we find it in Stanley's inarticulate "uh-gughh" and "caaahhh" at the end of *The Birthday Party,* in Edward's silent acceptance of the matchseller's tray in the closing moment of *A Slight Ache,* in Disson's catatonic collapse at the close of *Tea Party.* This also is the silence that gives its title to the play *Silence*—the silence of the gradual fading of memory, the gradual, inevitable dissolution of human personality itself.

To be filled, to be meaningful, Pinter's silences and pauses have to be meticulously *prepared:* only if the audience knows the possible alternative answers that might be given to a question can the absence of a reply acquire meaning and dramatic impact; only because we know what Disson might want to say—and the way in which he is torn between the conflicting desires and fears he is unable to keep under control—are we moved by his inability to speak. The effectiveness of the pauses and silences is, in Pinter's technique, the direct consequence of the density of texture of his writing: each syllable and each silence is part of an over-all design, all portions of which are totally integrated. Another way to put this would be to say that Pinter writes with the utmost economy, there are no redundant parts in his work. It is the economy by which a door, a simple ordinary door, can become a source of nameless fear and menace, merely because the character in the room has been shown to dread the intrusion of the outside world; the economy by which a character who has been kept silent through most of the play can cause an effect of overwhelming surprise by suddenly starting to speak; the economy of words that can invest the most threadbare cliché with hidden poetic meaning.

Teddy's departure in *The Homecoming* might be cited as a telling, final example of this supreme economy. Ruth, Teddy's wife, has consented to stay behind with the family and to become a prostitute. Teddy is returning to America alone. He has said goodbye to all the men in the room. He has not spoken to Ruth. He goes to the door. Then Ruth speaks: she calls him "Eddie."

Throughout the play Ruth has never addressed Teddy by his name. Talking to the others she has referred to him, as they have, as Teddy. The fact that she now calls him by a different name, the name that no doubt was the one she used when they were alone, thus acquires a particular force. "(*Teddy turns.*)" Quite clearly he feels that the use of a name Ruth regarded as part of their intimacy in earlier times, may indicate that she has changed her mind, that she may yet come with him. But having turned and having waited, he is greeted with silence. Pinter indicates a *pause*. Then Ruth merely says: "Don't become a stranger."

"Don't become a stranger" is a cliché, an idiom without any emotional force. It is what one says to a casual acquaintance after the holiday is over, the cruise has come to an end; if one were to explain the phrase in a dictionary of idioms one would translate it with no more than "We may meet again," or "See you some time." This, clearly, is also how Teddy understands it. For he goes and shuts the front door. Pinter indicates a *silence*. But in that silence, which concludes Teddy's visit, which sets a full stop to his appearance in the play and probably in the lives of the other characters, surely there will also echo something of the *literal* meaning of that phrase "Don't become a stranger," rather like a last despairing lament of a wife for the husband whom she has now lost, who has, in fact, at that very moment become a stranger to her.

Only five words, only eight syllables are actually spoken in that whole passage: "Eddie . . . Don't become a stranger." But through the surprise use of a name, through a pregnant pause and an utterly final silence, and through the subtle ambiguity of a phrase that is both a weak cliché and yet carries a strong literal meaning of deep, tragic impact, Pinter has put a wealth of drama, psychological profundity, suspense, irony, and pathos into those eight syllables.

Such economy and subtlety in the use of language, such density of subtext beneath the sparseness of the text itself, are surely the hallmarks of a real master of the craft of dialogue.

Pinter and Chekhov: The Bond of Naturalism

by John Lahr

> We begin with the idea that nature is all we need; it is necessary to accept her as she is, without modifying her or diminishing her in any respect; she is sufficiently beautiful and great to provide a beginning, a middle, and an end. Instead of imagining an adventure, complicating it, and arranging a series of theatrical effects to lead to a final conclusion, we simply take from life the story of a being or a group of beings whose acts we faithfully set down. The work becomes an official record, nothing more; its only merit is that of exact observation, of the more or less profound penetration of analysis, of the logical concatenation of facts. . . .
>
> "On Naturalism in the Theatre,"
> Emile Zola (1880)

Naturalism has its roots in a scientific approach which melds man inextricably to his environment, studying him as a complex amalgam of audible rhythms and spectacular mutations for survival. Chekhov, the passionate doctor, applied this discipline to the ailing conventional drama of his time.

> The demand is made that the hero and heroine should be dramatically effective. But in life people do not shoot themselves or hang themselves, or fall in love, or deliver themselves of clever sayings every minute. They spend most of their time eating, drinking, running after women or men, talking nonsense. It is therefore necessary that this should be shown on stage. A play ought to be written in which people

"Pinter and Chekhov: The Bond of Naturalism" by John Lahr. First published in *The Drama Review,* Vol. 13, no. 2 (T42—Winter 1968).

should come and go, dine, talk of the weather or play cards, not because the author wants it but because that is what happens in real life. Life on the stage should be as it really is, and the people, too, should be as they are and not on stilts.[1]

Although Chekhov was considerably influenced by Zola, his own poetic genius could not accept the Frenchman's dry book-keeping for the world. The same passion for objectivity and clinical analysis of the human animal which gives Chekhov so much of his strength feeds the work of Harold Pinter, who uses the conventions of Naturalism to go beyond them and chart mankind's evolving sense of its own boundaries.

Pinter, like Chekhov, has a scientist's distrust of simplifications. "I'm against all propaganda," he told Charles Marowitz in 1967, "Even propaganda for life." His realism refuses to offer bromidic meanings or strained coherence to palliate forces beyond our comprehension. This uncompromising aesthetic took shape even before Pinter began writing plays. Commenting on the work of Samuel Beckett in a letter (1954), he said:

. . . I don't want philosophies, tracts, dogmas, creeds, ways out, truths, answers, *nothing from the bargain basement.* He [Beckett] is the most courageous, remorseless writer going and the more he grinds my nose in the shit the more I am grateful to him. He's not fucking me about, he's not leading me up any garden, he's not slipping me any wink, he's not flogging me a remedy or a path or a revelation or a basinful of breadcrumbs, he's not selling me anything I don't want to buy, he doesn't give a bollock whether I buy or not, he hasn't got his hand over his heart. Well, I'll buy his goods, hook, line and sinker, because he leaves no stone unturned and no maggot lonely. . . .[2]

Pinter's impulse is for a supra-realism which can offer a vision of life in its ambiguous entirety, a theatrical hypothesis for an audience to entertain, in which all the facts are presented but never prejudged.

Man's dimensions of consciousness, his sense of a stable position in the scheme of things, have changed in this century. Chekhov, for all his hard-headed analysis, wrote out of a pastoral tradition to which

[1] Quoted in David Magarshack, *Chekhov the Dramatist* (New York: Hill & Wang, 1960), p. 84.

[2] *Beckett at Sixty* (London: Calder & Boyars, Ltd., 1967), p. 86.

the Russian gentry had become insensitive, one whose significance had been put into question by a new urban order. The stage directions of *The Cherry Orchard* (1903–1904) are explicit—

> A road leads to Gayev's estate. On one side and some distance away is a row of dark poplars, and it is there that the cherry orchard begins. Further away is seen a line of telegraph poles and beyond them, on the horizon, the vague outlines of a large town, visible only in very good, clear weather. . . .[3]

Chekhov's lyricism—a counterpoint of words, gestures and sound—is always within the larger matrix of the countryside. Pinter's world on the other hand is hermetically sealed off from nature. His plays are urban fables in which no poplars sway against the distant orchard, no wind underscores human loneliness. Man's earthly garden, like the one in *The Caretaker,* is cluttered with lifeless, alien objects.

> *Davies.* Looks a bit thick.
> *Aston.* Overgrown.
> *Davies.* What's that, a pond?
> *Aston.* Yes.
> *Davies.* What you got, fish?
> *Aston.* No. There isn't anything in there. (*Pause.*)
> *Davies.* Where are you going to put your shed?
> *Aston, turning.* I'll have to clear the garden first.
> *Davies.* You'd need a tractor, man.

When Pinter invokes Nature, it becomes a travesty, not only of pastoral simplicity, but of all those who would seek to recollect it in tranquility. In *The Birthday Party,* Goldberg tries and fails to make an innocent bower of London's East End:

> When I was a youngster, of a Friday I used to go for a walk down the canal with a girl who lived down my road. A beautiful girl. What a voice that bird had! A nightingale, my word of honor. Good? Pure? . . . We knew the meaning of respect. So I'd give her a peck and I'd bowl back home. I'd tip my hat to the toddlers, I'd give a helping hand to a couple of stray dogs, everything came natural! I can see it like yesterday. The sun falling behind the dog stadium. Ah!

[3] All Chekhov quotes are taken from: *Chekhov Plays,* translated by Elisaveta Fen (Penguin Books, 1954).

This blarney is sensual, precise, and vacuous. Nature has become a cynical ploy, a marginal diversion, a moment of verbal muscle-flexing which balloons it to the proportions of myth (as in Hemingway), substituting an unreal self-consciousness for Nature's inherent spontaneity.

In *The Seagull,* the lake is at first hidden by Treplev's wooden stage, an eclipse of nature by art significant for both Chekhov and his prototype of the young author. The play within the play is the embodiment of the romantic Egotistical Sublime—a stillborn creation if there ever was one. Treplev demands an organic, natural background for something coldly intellectual. This contrast is wryly humorous; but when the curtain comes up on his little play, the lake asserts an undeniable power. Chekhov's stage directions indicate the primordial calm of the background: "The curtain rises, revealing the view of the lake, with the moon above the horizon and its reflection in the water." This setting is perfect for Treplev's theme of cosmic death and rebirth. He will create a new Eden, with its animal delights and verdant profusion transposed from the external world into his own mind. Nina speaks Treplev's words against a background which reminds the audience that Nature still has something significant and sustaining to offer.

> The men, the lions, the eagles, the partridges, the antlered deer, the geese, the spiders, the silent fishes of the deep, starfishes and creatures unseen to the eye—in short all living things, all living things, having completed their mournful cycle, have been snuffed out . . . In me the consciousness of men is merged with the instincts of animals: I remember all, all, all, and live every single life anew in my own being. (I,i)

This speech is recalled by Nina in her last meeting with Treplev, stirring memories of a touching youthfulness and a talent never organized by a deeply-felt vision of the world. Treplev kills himself —the lie of romantic egotism now apparent even to him.

Even if they escape ultimate destruction, the characters in Chekhov's plays tend to ossify in their rural surroundings. Vanya, the three sisters, Arkadina reflect intellectual capacity turned flaccid: Astrov echoes Chekhov's sentiments:

> I love life as such—but our life, our everyday provincial life in Russia, I just can't endure. I despise it with all my soul. As for my own life, God knows I can find nothing good in it at all. You know,

> when you walk through a forest on a dark night and you see a small light gleaming in the distance you don't notice your tiredness, nor the darkness, nor the prickly branches lashing you in the face. . . . (II,i)

In Chekhov's world, the blessings of nature are omnipresent, but the majority of mankind are unable to mirror the peacefulness and potential grace which surrounds them. In *The Cherry Orchard,* the Ranevsky family are forced from their family estate by their own class pretensions. They exit to the thud of axes cutting the orchard, once the symbol of a luxuriant, safe world and now an accusation of their indifference to the environment which once sustained them. Even the final moments of *Uncle Vanya* reiterate this tension between the individual and nature. Sonia's sweet, vain longings are for an Eden whose visual correlative is outside her door.

> . . . We shall hear the angels, we shall see all the heavens covered with stars like diamonds, we shall see all earthly evil, all of our sufferings swept away by the grace which will fill the whole world, and our life will become peaceful, gentle, sweet as a caress. I believe it, I believe it. . . .

The watchman's tapping which fills the silence after Sonia's quiet pleading is the ironic Chekhovian smile. Sonia and Vanya are trapped; they cannot participate in Nature's tranquility. The boredom which pervades the life of Chekhov's characters has a palpable weight, an atmospheric pressure indicating their gradual withdrawal from the sustaining environment. One is, after all, never bored in nature as long as one can appreciate it.

Chekhov is writing, then, at the brink of a significant shift in man's attitude toward nature; his characters are both victims of its indifference and witnesses of its glory. This post-Darwinian ambivalence reverses former dramatic conventions of the pastoral. Country life in Russia does not bring the expected psychic release that Celia anticipates in *As You Like It* when she says, ". . . Now go we in content/To liberty and not to banishment." In Illyria or Arden, chaos is charmed into order, disguise and misconception are games which can be happily played out apart from the world. Chekhov revises the idyllic image, evoking complexity from the stereotype of pastoral security, creating a world which offers no fixed meaning, but only fading shadows of coherence.

It is significant that Stanislavski, unable to capture the strong interior rhythms of Chekhov or understand the momentum created by the counterpoint between situation and environment, wanted to clutter the plays with real things. The effect was to glut the imagination, blurring the careful delineation of objects and sounds Chekhov had indicated in his stage directions. Stanislavski's *mise-en-scène* for *Uncle Vanya* is indicative:

> The play starts in darkness; an August evening. The dim light of a lantern set on top of a post; distant sounds of a drunkard's song; distant howling of a dog; the croaking of frogs, the cry of a corncrake, the slow tolling of a distant church bell. All this helps the audience to get the feel of the sad and monotonous life of the characters. Flashes of lightning, faint rumblings of thunder in the distance. After the raising of the curtain a pause of ten seconds. After the pause, Yakov knocks, hammering in a nail (on the stage); having knocked the nail in, he busies himself on the stage, humming a tune.[4]

Chekhov's impressionistic technique demanded a more selectively focused *trompe d'oeil* effect, which tricked the audience into making thematic associations between characters and the sights and sounds surrounding them. The script reads simply: "The sun has just set. Yakov and other workmen are busy on the stage behind the lowered curtain; sounds of hammering and coughing."

Chekhov's careful choice of key objects, from Treplev's stuffed seagull to Vanya's elegant cravat, created a stagecraft oriented toward delicately accentuated things—a type of theatre from which Stanislavski could generalize a theory of performing. As Eric Bentley has observed in *In Search of Theatre,* the Chekhovian method

> . . . requires two extraordinary gifts: the mastery of "petty" realistic material and the ability to go beyond sheer *Sachlichkeit*—materiality, factuality—to imagination and thought . . . Now, the whole Stanislavski school of acting and directing is testimony that Chekhov was successfully *sachlich*—that is, not only accurate, but significantly precise, concrete, ironic . . . The art by which a special importance is imparted to everyday objects is familiar enough in fiction; on stage, Chekhov is one of its few masters. . . . (p. 333)

The breaking string, no matter how non-naturalistic a sound, has a human focus pertinence; the shimmering lake (*The Seagull*), the orchard flecked with May morning frost (*The Cherry Orchard*)

[4] David Magarshack, *Stanislavsky: a Life* (Chaunticleer Press, 1937), p. 172.

still uphold man as the measure of his environment, implying a kind of proportion to reality which lends humanity to objects clearly non-human. In contrast, the object world in Pinter is never so certain; it offers no sounds of general discord and comment—like the breaking string. Nature here allows no solace; the objects crowd with total indifference around Pinter's characters like the chest of drawers in Aston's room. His characters represent a modern consciousness wholly abstracted from its environment. The language, precise and sensual, tantalizes our sense of the real, only to disappear into the dynamics of the momentary situation. Max recalls a present to his wife in *The Homecoming:*

> . . . I said to her, Jessie, I think our ship is going to come home, I'm going to treat you to a couple of items, I'm going to buy you a dress in pale corded blue silk heavily encrusted in pearls, and for casual wear, a pair of pantaloons in lilac taffeta. Then, I gave her a drop of cherry brandy.

Language, however, cannot isolate the past, and neither can memory. Chekhov hints at this in *The Three Sisters*. Olga's first words show the limitations of the human imagination, trying to control facts which are irretrievable: "It's exactly a year ago Father died, isn't it?" The finality of the statement is mocked by the rhetorical question. In the same way, Max's childhood is never as clear as his memory urges it to be.

> Our father? I remember him. Don't worry. You kid yourself. He used to come over to me and look down at me. My old man did. He'd bend right over me, then he'd pick me up. I was only that big. Then he'd dandle me. Give me the bottle. Wipe me clean. Give me a smile. Pat me on the bum. Pass me around, pass me from hand to hand. Toss me up in the air. Catch me coming down. I remember my father.

The language seems sharply particular, but behind Max's ferocious certainty is a world of undifferentiated (perhaps false) shadows. He doesn't remember anything.

Pinter is obsessed by the arbitrary boundaries man makes for himself: the walls constructed of concrete, of language, of philosophy, which protect him from a protean reality and give him a chance. In one of his early plays, *The Dwarfs,* Pinter states what he later showed:

> The rooms we live in . . . open and shut . . . Can't you see? They change shape at their own will. I couldn't grumble if only they would keep to some consistency. But they don't. And I can't tell the limits, the boundaries which I've been led to believe are natural. . . .

In *The Birthday Party,* the house which has protected Stanley is turned into a menacing jungle. Pinter's attempts to transform the room are crude but effective. He throws the set into darkness during a game of blind man's buff, with the pursuers' flashlights scanning the room. The solidity evaporates. Objects become massive spectres in the dark, threatening to overwhelm the company. The light shines on them, assuring us that they exist, but the objects seem *less* than real. The walls protecting Stanley now incarcerate him, as Goldberg and McCann force a flashlight into his face until his solidity and reason vaporize. When Stanley is taken away, the room comes back to "normal," only to expand again into uncertainty with the final dialogue—

> *Meg.* I was the belle of the ball.
> *Petey.* Were you?
> *Meg.* Oh, it's true . . . I was . . . I know I was.

It is in *The Homecoming* that Pinter is able to achieve his most subtle interplay of naturalistic fact and a disturbing fluid reality. Max's living room seems as logical as the human situation within it seems improbable. The stage has been stripped of excess, lacking the jumbled and claustrophobic qualities of *The Caretaker* or the nonchalant untidiness of the seaside boarding house where *The Birthday Party* takes place. A mammoth arch, chairs, tables, the back wall broken through to expose a long staircase. The professor-son makes sure we, as well as his wife Ruth, realize this is a controlled environment.

> What do you think of the room? Big isn't it? It's a big house. I mean, it's a fine room, don't you think? Actually there was a wall, across there . . . with a door. We knocked it down . . . years ago . . . to make an open living area. The structure wasn't affected you see. . . .

The room seems certain to the eye, filled with a steel-gray light as solid and reassuring as a Vermeer painting. It is immediately recognizable; the objects coax the audience into a comfortable acceptance. The audience assumes that the surroundings describe the characters on stage. But their response is betrayed; the action uncovers elusive truths of sexual fantasy, lust, and impotence. As the play gathers momentum, the audience discovers—without Pinter forcing it—that the room has lost its apparent solidity. The stairway, covered by that monumental arch, takes on an unnatural, seductive, phallic length—an almost sexual potency.

Whereas Stanislavski developed the illusionistic "fourth wall" to give *The Seagull* the shock of reality, Pinter pushes against naturalistic stage conventions for his theatrical surprises. Sam, Max's aging brother, passes out, proclaiming in his last breath that Max's deceased wife committed adultery in the back seat of his cab while he drove. A plot-point is wrapped up; something is explained. But *The Homecoming* is not a play in which the dead are carted off. The dialogue is Pinter at his best, mocking the "realistic" demands of a theatre which hides man's most insensitive instincts.

> *Max.* What's he done? Dropped dead?
> *Lenny.* Yes.
> *Max.* A corpse on my floor. Clear him out of here.
> *Joey bends over Sam*
> *Joey.* He's not dead.
> *Lenny.* He's probably dead, for about 30 seconds.
> *Max.* He's not even dead.

The action goes on around the body. No blackouts. No fine sentiment. People faint in subways or die, other people pass them by or give them a nudge of the boot to make sure they're still breathing. Pinter lets reality comment on itself, never pointing a finger.

In Chekhov's world, the language comments on an environment which demands answers, resolved careers. In all his plays, there are voices that speak of happiness, that yearn for a better world. Even if these goals elude them, their mode of thinking about Nature and Man remains constructively anthropomorphic:

> But our sufferings may mean happiness for the people who come after us . . . There'll be a time when peace and happiness reign in the world, and then we shall be remembered kindly and blessed. . . .

Olga, like her sisters, waits for a sign from nature (". . . Maybe if we wait a little longer we shall find out why we live, why we suffer . . ."). Chekhov's own skepticism demanded both a world-view and hope.

> The best [classical writers] are realists and depict life as it is, because every line is permeated, as with a juice, by a conspicuousness of an aim; you feel in addition to life as it is life as it should be . . . But what about us? We depict life as it is but we refuse to go a step further. We have neither near nor remote aims and our souls are as flat and bare as a billiard table. We have no politics, we do not believe in revolution, we deny the existence of God, we are not afraid of ghosts . . . But he who wants nothing, hopes for nothing, and fears nothing cannot be an artist.[5]

Chekhov chronicles an existential stalemate, a problematic condition rather than a proposed answer. Yet there still remains the comforting solidity of possessions. Even though Lyuba Ranevsky loses her estate, the audience understands when she says, ". . . My dear bookcase! (*Kisses bookcase*). My own little table!" While symbols often emerge out of the dynamics of Chekhov's dramatic situations (Solyony's hands in *The Three Sisters,* the stuffed seagull, etc.), there is a logic in their use which, while attesting to the randomness of experience, confesses a comforting sense of artistic order. The object world of Chekhov's plays never imposes itself on the experience of the characters as much as on their imagination. In Pinter, objects and gestures take on a physical potency which illustrates a mute isolation between Man and object. Max swings his cane with a memory of sexual strength. Ruth weaves a mosaic of sensual innuendo, turning a glass of water into a throbbing organ:

> *Ruth.* Have a sip. Go on. Have a sip from my glass. *He is still.* Sit on my lap. Take a long cool sip. *She pats her lap. Pause. She stands, moves to him with the glass.* Put your head back and open your mouth.
>
> *Lenny.* Take that glass away from me.
>
> *Ruth.* Lie on the floor. Go on. I'll pour it down your throat.
>
> *Lenny.* What are you doing, making me some kind of proposal?

Lenny has tried to overwhelm her with tales of violence and sexual conquest. Ruth, however, by turning an object into a threatening invitation, mocks our faith in the neutrality of material things. She offers, one might say, an object lesson on the limitations of Man's sensory perception.

[5] David Magarshack, *Chekhov the Dramatist* (New York: Hill & Wang, 1960), pp. 40–41.

Look at me. I . . . move my leg. That's all it is. But I wear . . . underwear . . . which moves with me . . . it . . . captures your attention. Perhaps you misinterpret. The action is simple. It's a leg . . . moving. My lips move. Why don't you restrict . . . your observations to that? Perhaps the fact that they move is more significant . . . than the words which come through them. You must bear that . . . possibility . . . in mind.

Pinter's characters no longer cling to a wistful faith in cosmic coherence. They have been permanently cut adrift from their surroundings. They do not speak of Hope or Happiness; they simply want to survive from moment to moment. Where Chekhov explored the substance of man's life eroding through time, Pinter does something else with that dimension. All of Chekhov's characters come from a definable past, and their futures, no matter how bleak, can be charted. Irena will teach; Nina will act in the provinces; Gaev will take a job as a bank clerk. The language of Chekhov's plays at their most poignant moments is heightened by the future tense, by what *will be*. Futurity, like the "pathetic fallacy" of seeing nature responding to man, implies a relationship to the world, a chronological order, a sense of the mind's evolutionary development. Pinter employs no future tenses. His language shows memory a tractable tool, deceiving with seductive clarity. Memory holds no salvation and no value. Man can only live in an anxious, protracted present.

All Pinter's dramatic devices (the stylized speech, the weighted silences, the careful groupings) encompass the dicta of Nathalie Sarraute and the "new novel" which seeks, like Pinter's stage naturalism, to adapt to a modern environment. His drama moves where the novel (for her) must also go: ". . . some precise dramatic action shown in slow motion . . . [where] time was no longer the time of real life, but of a hugely amplified present . . ." [6]

Pinter finds the language of music the easiest way to describe his own understanding of his plays. Like Chekhov, he orchestrates an elaborate composition of gestures, words, and pauses within the flexible unit of the room. Chekhov had already used the pause with moving dramatic and psychological insight. Lyuba and Gaev's last moment before leaving the estate is made more touching by being beyond words. If Pinter's plays seem to lack the rich tonality of

[6] Gore Vidal, "French Letters," *Encounter* (December 1967), p. 19.

Chekhov's works, it is because, in his view, Nature gives us back no image of ourselves and words, no matter how sensuous, are finally imprecise. The actor works in a smaller, more tightly controlled area of improvisation. Pinter told me in 1967:

> I am very conscious of rhythm. It's got to happen "Snap. Snap"—just like that or it's wrong. I'm also interested in pitch . . . I remember when we did *The Collection* on Off-Broadway a few years ago, there was an American actor who was in big trouble with his part. I told him instead of trying to find reasons for his characterization, "Why don't you read the part and pay attention to the stress of the words." He did it, and he was fine. The point is the stresses tell you what the meaning is. Saying it up or down can change the whole meaning. It has to be just right.

Silence becomes a more active factor in modern life; the past has blurred and the future is unknowable. Pinter's plays exhibit a bold virtue in utilizing this silence, which Chekhov's Naturalism could only vaguely apprehend. It is a realistic device, as well as a cosmic indifference. As George Steiner has pointed out in *Language and Silence:* ". . . [when] language simply ceases, and the motion of the spirit gives no further outward manifestations of its being, the poet enters into silence. Here the word borders not on radiance or music, but on night."

Pinter, like Chekhov, uncovers a subterranean music. The difference in their techniques reflects the difference in evolving realistic appraisals of the world. If Pinter's world seems a smaller, grayer canvas, it is not a limitation of craft, but of the modern world—which leaves Man with less faith in his mind, more fearful of the dehumanizing forces outside it.

Taking Care of the Caretaker

by Valerie Minogue

A man went rushing into a building. "Fire! Fire! Fire!" he cried. "Hell! the flaming house is on fire!" Those who lived in the house had been trained in the New Criticism. "Splendidly vivid. Lower-class idiom," said one. "Repetitive but racy," said another. "Over-emotional of course, but dramatic," said a third. And they all went on with what they were doing. The funeral was a quiet affair.

This fable aptly represents the relations between Harold Pinter's play *The Caretaker,* and its critics. Although many have praised the production, the evocation of atmosphere, and the accurate reflection of lower-class talk, most have seen it as a sort of specialized sociological document. Few have explored the content and ideas of the play—these have been "taken care of" by being attributed to a "special belt of English suburbia."

Now that the play has been published (together with *The Birthday Party* and other plays in a companion volume[1]) we have little excuse for refusing to explore further. The plays require to be read by the mental vocal-cords rather than by the eye alone, but they are worth the effort.

In an interview on "Monitor" Pinter expressed his admiration for the lower-class speech with which he appears to have hypnotized the critics. He also objected, as I think justifiably, to the attitude of mind which relegates all the import of the play to a remote limbo solely inhabited by derelicts. What he admired about the idiom was its "muscularity"—and this seems to involve an attachment to the

"Taking Care of the Caretaker" by Valerie Minogue. From *The Twentieth Century,* 168 (September 1960), 243–48. Reprinted by permission of the author and *The Twentieth Century.*

[1] *The Caretaker* and *The Birthday Party and Other Plays,* by Harold Pinter (Methuen, 1960).

muscles of thought and feeling, from which the impulse to speak derives. This kind of talk is not formalized or pre-thought, not made into useful counters exchangeable at standard rates. Despite its apparent air of banality, and its inconsequences (or because of them) the effects are fresh and revealing. Even the worn-out cliché creates its own horror, when we see its ineptness at the very moment of utterance:

> "I never had enough time to go into it," [says the tramp; or again, watching Aston fiddling with a plug]:
> "You getting to the root of the trouble are you?"
> "I've got a suspicion."
> "You're lucky."

The difference between this and middle-class speech seems less one of kind than of degree. Middle-class speech less often reveals its lacunas, and though it also derives from the rag-bag and pot-pourri of jargon and cliché, appearances are better kept up. The merest twitch of a toe may be the only expression of the sudden discomfort. In *The Caretaker,* discomforts, evasions, and pretensions flash like headlights on a dark road.

In the three characters, the illusions are less expertly integrated, the supposed realities less solidly entrenched, the fears, confusions, and delusions of grandeur nearer the surface than they are in most of us. Clearly this idiom, and this group of people served Mr Pinter's purpose particularly well—but what purpose? Only the writer himself can tell us; but we can at least examine what he has done, and discuss his achievement.

Three men are trying, by means of language, to surmount barriers and find common ground. Their language itself, because of its imperfections—and their lack of expertise—reveals the fears, needs, and inadequacies they struggle to conceal. All three co-operate to cover up things which are embarrassing not merely to one but to all. They attempt to close the abyss—silence is the great enemy—generally understanding too much rather than too little. Their talk shows, as Mr Pinter said, not so much a failure as an evasion of communication. In silence, the questions they avoid are deafening, and silence in this world becomes a catalyst of action, even action itself. Talk seems an expedient, a means of evasion. In silence and in the dark is the nonentity against which they all precariously struggle.

The fight against nonentity, or simply non-being, is something that echoes over and over through the Pinter plays. In *The Birthday Party,* Goldberg and McCann taunt Webber with

> "Who are you, Webber? What makes you think you exist?"

and this is a repetition of Stan's enquiry, early in the play (moving typically from the phrase "who do you think you're talking to?"):

> "Tell me, Mrs Boles, when you address yourself to me, do you ever ask yourself who exactly you are talking to?"

In the case of the tramp of *The Caretaker,* who has left all his papers at Sidcup, the theme is worked out against the background of the other two men, who have a slightly stronger grip on identity. Aston achieves this by clinging tightly to the very little he has left, and Mick by refusing to let anything come between him and his "I'll-make-this-place-into-a-penthouse" delusions of grandeur.

Pinter's analytical use of the idiom, betraying at each moment the bare bones of motive and emotion, is often funny, but also embarrassing, and at times, unbearable. Kenneth Tynan, reviewing the play, wrote "one laughs in recognition; but one's laughter is tinged with snobbism." This seems to indicate an enviable certainty of being out of reach. It would be comforting if this picture of humanity had nothing to do with the world we know, but it seems to concern not an isolated group of institutionalized eccentrics, but Man in general. If my laughter was tinged with anything, it was embarrassment, and occasionally horror, a feeling of having been caught out, and exposed to a chill wind.

To relegate this comment on life to a special and defined area is in many ways a sensible protective reaction; it is difficult to live without some regard for mental comfort. Pinter's view may be salutary, but it is far from pleasant. It forces upon us standards of judgement by which we cannot live, awareness that we would sooner avoid. To see human helplessness, to recognize the vainglorious weakness with which we habitually meet facts and situations that appal if seen too clearly—this is to hold up a mirror to an aspect of life (not total but none the less true) which it is easier to ignore than contemplate.

Does no one wonder, hearing Aston's description of his experiences in a mental hospital, and seeing the curious halflife he leads, whether there is not something wrong, and perhaps a little cocksure about our treatment of those we regard as of unsound mind? Does no one recognize in himself the hapless turning from attitude to attitude in order to entrench a position, or see, in the desperate claims to knowing what goes on, his own baffled attempts to lay claim to at least a partial understanding of what life is all about? Does no one share the feeling that "if only the weather would break," if only everyone and everything would stand still for a tick of time (in fact if only things were different) then one might have a chance? Does no one see in Aston's sad monologue, his own reduction by the shocks of living; does no one feel appalled at the difficulties of disinterested kindness in a world that lives not by charity but by politics?

We have all left our references and papers somewhere. We mostly feel we have "cards of identity" somewhere even more inaccessible than Sidcup. Sidcup seems to derive from the same myth-making impulse as the Garden of Eden, where we mislaid our innocence and our nobility, but if the weather would break, we might dash back and get them—but,

> The glass is falling hour by hour, the glass will fall for ever, But
> if you break the bloody glass you won't hold up the weather.

One sees in the play the frenzied attempt to feel important, and to be "in" on things. We must know the right responses whether to jig-saws, fret-saws, "Blacks," work-shy people, the latest "ism" or the newest West End play. We must know what "they" are saying, even if we choose to disagree. "Oh, they're handy," says the tramp, and we recognize the awful futility of it all. The terrible thing about the dialogue is that it has the authentic ring of the stop-gap. Behind it lies the awareness of another world of meanings, a plane on which defeats are being acknowledged, and where there is a fight for the right to exist, an endless apology for existence, a fierce assertion of rights, and a hideous plea for forgiveness of what is known to be unforgivable, and irremediable. When silence begins to leak through the battered pores of the speakers, they point to the obvious, to the bucket for instance, catching the drips from the roof. They distract each other's attention away to the mundane realities, that are at the same time a symbol of the unsatisfactory state of things which will, of course, be put right in time, when the shed is built in the garden, when we get back from Sidcup with our papers.

Or again, when the silence threatens, one may ask "What's your name?" and continue the fight against nonentity. No matter that it's been asked before, and given before; it's still a symbol of stability, especially if we know not only the assumed name, but the *real* name as well. Yet it tells us nothing. Anonymity remains, and the papers are still at Sidcup. We are all in some sense dispossessed, frightened, ridiculous, like the tramp who, in the bravado of fear, pulls out a knife against Mick. Mick sits beside him when he is bored with baiting him, and offers him a sandwich. They sit together, getting chummy over shared views, while the tramp, who appears to have no views, tries to commit himself to views acceptable to Mick. Mick, taking the intention as sufficient, says "I can see you're a man of the world," thus acknowledging the tramp's right to exist in the world he is a man of. And we are all in this sense "men of the world" claiming to know what is going on in a world dominated by "them." We too have our fingers on the imaginary pulse of things, we know there is a "crying need" for this, that, and the other. We have to have some pipe-line to "in-ness" if not to infinity. We like to tap our heads significantly like Mr Pinter's tramp implying that "they" haven't got *us* fooled. And it all underlines our helplessness in a world even more obviously out of control than usual.

We pretend to know what it all means, and jockey for position in a competitive world whose rules are baffling. We resemble the tramp whose shifts of allegiance, whose endless search for the expedient are pitilessly laid bare. We see his vain efforts to discover exactly where his dependence lies; he wants clearly to know "which way the wind is blowing," and spends a great deal of time trying to find absolute answers to the question—who has the power to kick him out? Whose support does he need most? It seems ultimately his servility that defeats him, for servility implies at least some knowledge of whom it is worthwhile to placate. When this proves impossible to discover, he has no means of living with the others. He goes off at the end of the play, presumably to find other people on whom to impose his failures, his trailing clouds of vainglory, others to whom he can justify himself—perhaps searching for a day of judgement, but unable to find a judge. It is interesting that at the end, Aston stands with his back to him, refusing to speak, refusing to see him, and slowly the tramp's efforts to talk himself into recognition twitter away into the long silence in which he recognizes defeat.

No one is much interested in forgiving or condemning him, no one wants to know the "truth" about him, no one wants his excuses or promises, for they have their own, and so have we all.

While Mick, the younger brother, is a bundle of undirected energies, flexing his muscles, but achieving nothing, it is Aston, the gentle elder brother who has authority. This appears to derive from his having his silences under control. He has accepted defeat, recognized limitations, and impotence, as though he had been surgically detached from his life, while Mick and the tramp are still shadow-boxing with theirs. When, at the end of a fierce scene with the tramp, he announces quietly, "I don't think we're hitting it off," it seems not merely understated, but under-experienced, only half-felt. He seems almost emotionless, though he recognizes occasional discomforts and seeks to remove them. He accepts the abyss as normal, nonentity as a mode of existence, and lives in a permanently shell-shocked state where his own reality is without importance. He seems more able to cope with immediate things than the other two, perhaps because he is so uninvolved. One may well ask whether reality is so terrible that one can only accept it by losing half one's life. The half that is left is capable of registering surprise; he has some sense of the fitness of things, while the tramp, completely enclosed in fantasy, does not even have this. Aston's concern about building the shed before he begins to decorate is far less aggressive than the excuses of the other two. One feels that he knows he's beaten before he begins, but it doesn't much matter anyway. The shed-illusion seems at times a polite piece of conformism—a way of sharing the life and idiom of the others.

Now all of this seems far more than a specialized sociological study, and involves more than the pleasure of recognizing conversations overheard in buses and public places. Certainly it is possible we may ultimately have to avoid the issue, but we might first look at what we are about to evade.

There is little point in pretending that Mr Pinter had nothing to say to us anyway. When someone shouts "Fire!" it's fun to analyse the style, but it may not be prudent to ignore the content.

The World of Harold Pinter

by Ruby Cohn

Each of Harold Pinter's four plays ends in the virtual annihilation of an individual. In Pinter's first play, *The Room,* after a blind Negro is kicked into inertness, the heroine, Rose, is suddenly stricken with blindness. In *The Dumb Waiter,* the curtain falls as Gus and his prospective murderer stare at each other. Stanley Webber, the hero of *The Birthday Party,* is taken from his refuge for "special treatment." In *The Caretaker,* the final curtain falls on an old man's fragmentary (and unheeded) pleas to remain in his refuge.

As Pinter focuses more sharply on the wriggle for existence, each of his successive hero-victims seems more vulnerable than the last. Villain assaults victim in a telling and murderous idiom. Although Pinter's first two plays are in one act, and the second two in three acts, each successive drama seems to begin closer to its own end, highlighting the final throes of the hero-victims.

But who are they—these nondescript villains and victims, acting out their dramas in dilapidated rooms? Victims emerge from a vague past to go to their ineluctable destruction. Villains are messengers from mysterious organizations—as in the works of Kafka or Beckett.

If Pinter has repeatedly been named as Beckett's heir on the English stage, it is because the characters of both lead lives of complex and unquiet desperation—a desperation expressed with extreme economy of theatrical resources. The clutter of our world is mocked by the stinginess of the stage-worlds of Beckett and Pinter. Sets, props, characters, and language are stripped by both playwrights to what one is tempted to call their essence.

However, Pinter is not only Beckett's spiritual son. He is at least a cousin of the Angry Young Englishmen of his generation, for

"The World of Harold Pinter" by Ruby Cohn. First published in *Tulane Drama Review,* Vol. 6, no. 3 (T15—March 1962).

Pinter's anger, like theirs, is directed vitriolically against the System. But his System cannot be reduced to a welfare state, red brick universities, and marriage above one's class. Of all the Angries, John Wain approaches closest to Pinter's intention when he states that the artist's function "is always to *humanize* the society he is living in, to assert the importance of humanity in the teeth of whatever is currently trying to annihilate that importance" (*Declaration*). Pinter's assertion, however, takes a negative form; it is by his bitter dramas of *de*humanization that he implies "the importance of humanity." The religion and society which have traditionally structured human morality, are, in Pinter's plays, the immoral agents that destroy the individual.

Like Osborne, Pinter looks back in anger; like Beckett, Pinter looks forward to nothing (not even Godot). Pinter has created his own distinctive and dramatic version of Man vs. the System. Situating him between Beckett and the Angries is only a first approximation of his achievement.

The house as human dwelling is a metaphor at least as old as the Bible, and on the stage that house is most easily reduced to a room (e.g., Graham Greene's *Living Room,* Beckett's *Endgame*). Pinter's rooms are stuffy, nonspecific cubes, whose atmosphere grows steadily more stale and more tense. The titular Room of his first play is "A room in a large house"; in *The Dumb Waiter,* we descend to "a basement room"; in *The Birthday Party,* we have "The living room of a house in a seaside town," and, in *The Caretaker,* it is simply "A room." Unlike the tree and road of *Godot,* which suggest vegetation and distance; or the shelter of *Endgame,* which looks out on earth and sea; unlike the realistic "one-room flat . . . at the top of a large Victorian house" of *Look Back in Anger,* Pinter's rooms, parts of mysterious and infinite series, are like cells without a vista. At the opening curtain, these rooms look naturalistic, meaning no more than the eye can contain. But by the end of each play, they become sealed containers, virtual coffins.

Within each Pinter room, the props seem to be realistically functional, and only in retrospect do they acquire symbolic significance. Consider, for example, Pinter's treatment of such crucial details as food and clothing, in comparison with the casual realism of Osborne, or the frank symbolism of Beckett. The various preparations for tea in *Look Back in Anger* seem to be parallelled by the prosaic cocoa, tea, bread, sandwiches, crackers of Pinter's plays; in sharp contrast is the farcical and stylized carrot-turnip-radish "business" of *Godot*. So too, three men grabbing for an old man's bag in *The Caretaker* has few of the symbolic overtones of the slapstick juggling of derbies in *Godot*.

It is, however, in their respective use of that innocuous prop, a pair of shoes, that the different symbolic techniques of Beckett and Pinter are in most graphic evidence. Early in *Godot,* Vladimir establishes shoes as a metaphysical symbol: "There's man all over for you, blaming on his boots the faults of his feet." At the end of *Godot,* it is by virtue of being barefoot that Estragon admits he has always compared himself to Christ. In Pinter's *Caretaker,* the old man keeps trying on different shoes that might enable him to get on the road to Sidcup, where he claims to have left his identity papers. Each pair of shoes is rejected for specific misfit—"a bit small," "too pointed," "no laces"—before the curtain-lines of the play: "they're all right . . . if I was to . . . get my papers . . . would you . . . would you let . . . would you . . . if I got down . . . and got my. . . ." The finality of the fragments indicates that no shoes can ever fit, that the journey to Sidcup cannot be made. Thus, the symbolic significance of the shoes is instantaneous with Beckett, cumulative with Pinter.

Most crucial to an understanding of Pinter's theatre is the symbolism of his characters. For all their initially realistic appearance, their cumulative impact embraces the whole of humanity. In so generalizing, Pinter extends the meaning of his characters beyond such particulars as Osborne treats; nevertheless, he does not achieve the metaphysical scope upon which Beckett insists, from his opening lines: "Nothing to be done."

Pinter's defenseless victims are a middle-aged wife, a man who asks too many questions, an ex-pianist, a broken old man. Ruthlessly robbed of any distinction, they come to portray the human condition. And Pinter's villains, initially as unprepossessing as the victims, gradually reveal their insidious significance through some of the most skillful dialogue on the English stage today. For it is language that betrays the villains—more pat, more cliché-ridden, with more brute power than that of their victims.

Even hostile critics have commented on the brilliance of Pinter's dialogue, and it is in the lines of his villains that he achieves precise dramatic timing and economical manipulation of commonplaces. Representatives of the System, Pinter's villains give direct expression to its dogma. In the plays of Osborne and Beckett, which also implicitly attack the System, the oppressive forces are presented through the words of their victims.

Jimmy Porter of Osborne's *Look Back in Anger* garbs the System in contemporary corporate metaphors:

> *Jimmy Porter.* . . . the Economics of the Supernatural. It's all a simple matter of payments and penalties . . . Reason and Progress, the old firm, is selling out. Everyone get out while the going's good. Those forgotten shares you had in the old traditions, the old beliefs are going up—up and up and up. There's going to be a changeover. A new Board of Directors, who are going to see that the dividends are always attractive, and that they go to the right people. Sell out everything you've got; all those stocks in the old, free inquiry. The Big Crash is coming, you can't escape it, so get in on the ground floor with Helena and her friends while there's still time. And there isn't much of it left. Tell me, what could be more gilt-edged than the next world! It's a capital gain, and it's all yours.

Vladimir and Estragon, at the beginning of Beckett's *Godot,* describe the invisible deity figure in trivial human terms:

> *Vladimir.* Let's wait and see what he says.
> *Estragon.* Who?
> *Vladimir.* Godot.
> *Estragon.* Good idea.
> *Vladimir.* Let's wait till we know exactly how we stand.
> *Estragon.* On the other hand it might be better to strike the iron before it freezes.
> *Vladimir.* I'm curious to hear what he has to offer. Then we'll take it or leave it.
> *Estragon.* What exactly did we ask him for? . . . And what did he reply?
> *Vladimir.* That he'd see.
> *Estragon.* That he couldn't promise anything.
> *Vladimir.* That he'd have to think it over.
> *Estragon.* In the quiet of his home.
> *Vladimir.* Consult his family.
> *Estragon.* His friends.
> *Vladimir.* His agents.

Estragon. His correspondents.
Vladimir. His books.
Estragon. His bank account. . . . Where do we come in?
Vladimir. Come in?
Estragon. Take your time.
Vladimir. Come in? On our hands and knees.

In Pinter's *Birthday Party,* Goldberg and McCann express the System by echoing modern commonplaces of social success. Pinter damns them with their own deadly clichés.

Goldberg. Between you and me, Stan, it's about time you had a new pair of glasses.
McCann. You can't see straight.
Goldberg. It's true. You've been cockeyed for years.
McCann. Now you're even more cockeyed.
Goldberg. He's right. You've gone from bad to worse.
McCann. Worse than worse.
Goldberg. You need a long convalescence.
McCann. A change of air.
Goldberg. Somewhere over the rainbow.
McCann. Where angels fear to tread. . . .
Goldberg. We'll make a man of you.
McCann. And a woman.
Goldberg. You'll be re-orientated.
McCann. You'll be rich.
Goldberg. You'll be adjusted.
McCann. You'll be our pride and joy.
Goldberg. You'll be a mensch.
McCann. You'll be a success.
Goldberg. You'll be integrated.
McCann. You'll give orders.
Goldberg. You'll make decisions.
McCann. You'll be a magnate.
Goldberg. A statesman.
McCann. You'll own yachts.
Goldberg. Animals.
McCann. Animals.

In comparing the three excerpts, we note that Osborne's sustained metaphors are almost lyrical with rebellion, but both Beckett and Pinter resort to pithy stichomythia. Although the passages are typical of the technique of each play, the respective tonal differences depend upon the dramatic structure. Osborne's satiric hostility recurs throughout *Look Back in Anger,* but Beckett's attitude towards Godot is ambivalent. The quoted excerpt occurs early in the play, when the tramps, in spite of their pathetic plight, can still attempt to define the System in familiar human terms. But by the end of the drama, man and deity are poignantly reduced to their compulsive, impossible, problematical interrelationship: "in this immense confusion one thing alone is clear," says Vladimir. "We are waiting for Godot to come."

In the Pinter play, the messengers of the System glibly mouth its pat phrases—increasingly pointed as the dehumanization of the victim progresses. In the quoted excerpt, which occurs towards the end of the drama, the seemingly irrelevant conclusion, "Animals," corrosively climaxes the process.

The central victim-villain conflict may be traced through Pinter's four plays. In the one-act *Room,* where the presentation of the human dilemma is somewhat diffuse, victim and villain are recognized as such only at the final curtain. Rose and Bert Hudd, wife and husband, alone onstage when the play begins, are almost alone when the curtain falls—except for the still body of the blind Negro, whose head Bert has kicked against the stove. But it is Rose who is Bert's victim, Rose whose suffering is sustained throughout the play, Rose who is suddenly and finally afflicted with the Negro's blindness.

When the play opens, Rose is busy preparing a realistic tea in their realistic room, while Bert Hudd quietly reads a realistic newspaper. Bert's silence in the face of Rose's disconnected rambling, seems to be a lower-class, marital-comedy silence. When Mr. Kidd, the landlord, enters to look at the pipes, to converse with husband and wife, Bert's persistent and insistent silence takes on a threatening quality. Mr. Kidd talks about the house, about the time he used to live in their room. Quite suddenly, room and inhabitants lose their humdrum exterior, and take on new depth. When Rose asks how many floors there are in the house, Mr. Kidd replies, "Well, to tell you the truth, I don't count them now."

Close upon this rejection of the numerable, Mr. Kidd reminisces about his dead sister, his Jewish mother. There is a sporadic return to small talk, as Mr. Kidd admires Bert Hudd's van, his driving. After Mr. Kidd leaves, Bert Hudd, in increasingly sinister silence, goes down to his van. During his absence, a Mr. and Mrs. Sands come looking for a room; a man in the basement has told them there was one for rent. There is a confused conversation about the landlord, whom Mr. Sands mixes up with Bert, since the names Hudd and Kidd sound alike. Rose's security is shaken, and she denies the rumor of a vacancy. Mr. Sands insists that the man in the basement has offered them number seven—Rose's room.

When the Sands couple leaves, carrying with them all hint of social satire, the surface plausibility of the dialogue collapses completely. When Mr. Kidd reenters, Rose pounces upon him to affirm her claim to the room. But Mr. Kidd can talk only of a mysterious man in the basement, who has been waiting for Bert Hudd to leave, so that he can come up to see Rose. Even as she denies any knowledge of the man, she consents to see him. When a blind Negro enters, Rose screams that she doesn't know him, that his name is not Riley, as he claims. Riley announces his message: "Your father wants you to come home." Calling her Sal, Riley soon shifts to, "*I* want you to come home." [My italics] After Riley's final, "Come home now, Sal," Bert Hudd returns to the room, and speaks for the first time. In short, harsh sentences, he describes driving his van through the cold streets: "She took me there. She brought me back." When Riley addresses him, "Mr. Hudd, your wife—," Bert cries, "Lice!" He knocks Riley down and kicks his head until he lies still. Rose stands clutching her eyes, moaning, "Can't see. I can't see. I can't see."

Of the rival claimants for Rose, Riley and Bert, the latter bludgeons his way to triumph. Bert's role as villain explodes climactically, for it is Riley who first appears to menace Rose. But silence, conventional connubial demands, and a van (female in Bert's lines) are victorious over the blind Negro father-surrogate. Earlier, the landlord, Mr. Kidd, is nearly driven "off his squiff" by Riley's insistence on seeing Rose. With Bert, however, Mr. Kidd seems to have reached a *modus vivendi,* even though Bert never addresses him. Mr. Kidd admires Bert's driving ability; he too speaks of the van as a woman. Their very names, Kidd and Hudd, sound so much alike that outsiders such as the Sands, confuse them with one another. It is the presence of Riley against which both Kidd and Hudd react—the former with terror, the latter with violence. Although Riley is kicked unconscious by Bert, it is Rose-Sal who is

Bert's ultimate prey. "A woman of sixty," garrulous and shuffling, she speaks disparagingly of foreigners, dwells on her physical comforts, is ungracious to the Sands, and hostile to Riley. At the last, she makes no attempt to defend Riley from Bert, but succumbs to her own blindness. Pinter has stripped her of all appealing qualities, so that any sympathy she inspires must be rooted in her plight.

Pinter's second play, the one-act *The Dumb Waiter,* concentrates even more pointedly on the plight of the victim. As in *The Room,* it is not immediately evident who is victim and who villain. Sent by an offstage Wilson "to do a job," Gus and Ben, the play's two characters, await instructions in a basement room which contains two beds separated by a hatch—a dumb-waiter. While they wait, Gus busies himself with preparations for a realistic tea, and Ben reads the bloodier items from a realistic newspaper. Their life seems to lie in their Kafka-like career; as Gus summarizes it, "you come into a place when it's still dark, you come into a room you've never seen before, you sleep all day, you do your job, and then you go away in the night again." [1]

Despite the menace implicit in the job itself, early disquieting signs are plausible by their very triviality: the toilet has a deficient ballcock, the bed sheets are dirty, Gus and Ben cannot see a football game because all teams are playing "away." After an envelope of matches is mysteriously slipped under the door, they quarrel tensely about whether one can say "light the kettle," or must say "light the gas." Gus unobtrusively asks a few questions of Ben, "the senior partner." The gas goes out before their water boils, and Gus begins to have mutinous thoughts about Wilson, their boss. He thinks with distaste of their last job, a girl who was "a mess"; he wonders who cleans up after their jobs. "It was that girl made me start to think—," Gus reflects, and is interrupted by a sudden noise from the dumb-waiter. In a box is a note ordering "Two braised steak and chips." One by one, other notes are sent down the dumb-waiter,

[1] Compare this description with that of Jimmy Porter's naturalistic Sundays in *Look Back in Anger*: "Always the same ritual. Reading the papers, drinking tea, ironing. A few more hours, and another week gone. Our youth is slipping away."

On the other hand, observe Vladimir's clearly metaphysical routine in *Godot*: "Tomorrow, when I wake, or think I do, what shall I say of today? That with Estragon my friend, at this place, until the fall of night, I waited for Godot? That Pozzo passed, with his carrier, and that he spoke to us? Probably. But in all that what truth will there be?"

requesting an international series of delicacies. By the dumb-waiter, Gus sends up their meager tea supplies, comically and sadly prosaic in the vulgarity of modern brand names: "Three McVitie and Price! One Lyons Red Label! One Eccles cake! One Fruit and Nut!" Ben, "the senior partner," quickly corrects the Fruit and Nut to "Cadbury's."

This task accomplished, Ben conducts their preparations for the job; he superintends their attire and the cleaning of their revolvers. Through a suddenly discovered speaking tube, he apologizes that they have nothing more to send up the dumb-waiter. Humbly, he listens to the complaints about their service: "The Eccles cake was stale . . . The chocolate was melted . . . The milk was sour . . . The biscuits were mouldy." Then, triumphantly, Ben reports that they have been ordered to light the kettle: "Not put on the kettle!. Not light the gas! But light the kettle!" However, there is still no gas.

In final rehearsal for the job, they recite their instructions about the victim:

> *Gus.* He won't say a word.
> *Ben.* He'll look at us.
> *Gus.* And we'll look at him.
> *Ben.* Nobody says a word.

Gus goes to the toilet a last time. "The lavatory chain is pulled . . . but the lavatory does not flush." When Gus returns, he reiterates his uneasy questions until Ben strikes him. The dumb-waiter tray clatters down; hysterically, Gus reads, "Scampi."

Ben returns to his newspaper, and Gus exits for a glass of water. As Ben waits, the toilet flushes belatedly, and Ben cries, "Gus!"

> The door right opens sharply. Ben turns, his revolver levelled at the door. Gus stumbles in. He is stripped of his jacket, waistcoat, tie, holster and revolver. He stops, body stooping, his arms at his sides. He raises his head and looks at Ben. A long silence. They stare at each other. Curtain.

It is because he has not been content to be a "dumb waiter" that Gus is destroyed. Although only a junior partner, perhaps *because* he is only a junior partner, he has complained about the job, and begun to ask questions; he has found Wilson "hard to talk to," has even meant to ask questions of him. But the organization turns upon Gus before he can probe or expose it.

Until his first three-act play, *The Birthday Party,* the threats in Pinter's drama emanate mysteriously from a vague apparatus of master-messenger-organization. But with his third play, Pinter not only defines the enemy more explicitly, but casts a restrospective light upon the villains of the earlier plays. Goldberg and McCann, who represent the System in *The Birthday Party,* do not appear on scene until the end of the first act, and until they do, the living room of the Boles' boardinghouse is Pinter's most photographically real set. Although Stanley Webber's reaction against the two prospective boarders seems disproportionate, and his review of his earlier concert career ambiguous, we do not definitively leave the realistic surface until Goldberg and McCann actually enter by the back door. Partners like Ben and Gus, they carry no revolvers, but pose as casual vacationers in the seaside boardinghouse where Stanley has taken refuge. Their first monosyllabic exchange establishes their relationship:

McCann. Is this it?
Goldberg. This is it.
McCann. Are you sure?
Goldberg. Sure I'm sure.

Their Jewish-Irish names and dialects suggests a vaudeville skit, and it is not long before we realize that that skit is the Judaeo-Christian tradition as it appears in our present civilization. Goldberg is the senior partner; he utters the sacred clichés of family, class, prudence, proportion. McCann is the brawny yes-man whose strength reënforces Goldberg's doctrine.

Although Meg and Petey Boles have sheltered Stanley in their home, they are unable to recognize that the sinister new guests threaten the welfare of their guest. Meg acquiesces joyously to Goldberg's suggestion of a birthday party for Stanley "to bring him out of himself." Villains and victim, Goldberg-McCann and Stanley are not brought face to face in Act I, but Stanley already begins to feel trapped.

Before the party that fills Act II, Stanley tries to convince McCann that he is not "the sort of bloke to—to cause any trouble," that it is all a mistake, that Goldberg and McCann have to leave because their room is rented. Having forced Stanley to sit down, Goldberg and, secondarily, McCann engage in a verbal fencing-match with Stanley, in which Pinter parodies the contemporary emptiness of the Judaeo-Christian heritage.

Interrupting Stanley's efforts at self-defense, Meg comes down ready for the party. In the maudlin mixture of drinking, pawing, and reminiscing that follows, a game of Blindman's Buff is played. An increasingly desperate Stanley tries to strangle Meg, a mother-surrogate, and rape Lulu, the sexy neighbor, but Goldberg and McCann advance upon him each time. As Act II closes, "[Stanley's] giggle rises and grows as he flattens himself against the wall. Their [Goldberg and McCann] figures converge upon him."

Act III is a virtual *post mortem*. Goldberg, McCann, and Petey talk about Stanley's "nervous breakdown." McCann complains to Goldberg about this job, and Goldberg encourages him by an interweaving of clichés, in which the Biblical tradition is the warp, and modern success formulas the woof: "Play up, play up, and play the game. Honour thy father and thy mother. All along the line. Follow the line, the line, McCann, and you can't go wrong."

When McCann finally ushers Stanley down, "dressed in striped trousers, black jacket, and white collar," the victim has lost the power of speech, and his glasses are broken. Again, Goldberg and McCann attack him verbally, in even pithier phrases, but this time they promise him worldly success if he complies. Stanley only gurgles unintelligibly.

"Still the same old Stan," Goldberg pronounces, and he and McCann start to lead Stanley to an unexplained Monty. When Petey Boles objects that Stanley can stay on at the boardinghouse, the macabre pair scornfully invite Petey to join them, "Come with us to Monty. There's plenty of room in the car." An automaton propped between the partners, Stanley is helped out while Petey, broken-hearted, calls, "Stan, don't let them tell you what to do!" But Goldberg's car is heard starting up, then fading into the distance. When Meg Boles comes down with a morning hangover, Petey does not even tell her Stan is gone, but encourages her to dream of the birthday party, at which she was the "belle of the ball."

The thread running through all Pinter's plays now appears more clearly. If we recall *The Room* in the light of *The Birthday Party*, we see resemblances between Goldberg and Mr. Kidd, who had a

Jewish mother. Both emphasize the value of property, of progress, of family, of tradition. Similarly, the Irish names of Riley and McCann seem to indicate a Christian continuance of the Judaic legacy; in both plays, they are the weaker members, although never as weak as Gus of *The Dumb Waiter,* who is metamorphosed into a victim.

In *The Birthday Party* and *The Dumb Waiter,* there is a higher, invisible power behind the messengers, but Monty remains even more mysterious than Wilson, and more authority is invested in Goldberg than in Ben. In all the plays, the motor van becomes a clear symbol of modern power. In the first play, *The Room,* the van belongs to Bert Hudd, but is the object of Mr. Kidd's admiration. In *The Birthday Party,* as in *The Dumb Waiter,* the van is the property of one of the messengers—in each case, of the dominant and senior partner. It seems to be the older, crueler tradition which best embraces modern mechanization. Only the recalcitrant individual must be quashed.

As the victim-villain conflict in *The Room* is somewhat diffused by the socially satirized Sands couple, so the Boles couple in *The Birthday Party* provides a comic relief from the mounting tension. And yet the latter couple functions more directly in the symbolic context, for the Boles are not, like Mr. Kidd, mere landlords; they provide a temporary if tawdry refuge for Stanley. Distasteful as are the attentions of Meg-mother-mistress, impersonal as is Petey's presence, the Boles express affection and concern for Stanley. But human emotions are tricked or brushed aside by the ruthless team of a dogmatic system.

In Pinter's latest play, *The Caretaker,* as in the earlier *The Dumb Waiter,* there are no deflections from the hunting down of victim by villain. Although none of Pinter's victims are sentimentalized—Rose is gruff, Gus has performed bloody deeds before he has begun to question them, Stanley is ungrateful to Meg—the old man of *The Caretaker* is perhaps the least sympathetic of all. He is ready to take anything from anyone, he feels superior to "them Blacks," he is suspicious of everyone, he repeatedly complains that the weather prevents his going to Sidcup for the papers which he left there during the war, and which can establish his identity.

After the opening tableau of *The Caretaker,* in which the leather-jacketed Mick slowly examines the miscellaneous objects in the room, Mick exits when he hears voices. Aston enters in worn but conventional clothes, and after him comes the ragged old man, "following, shambling, breathing heavily." Thrown out of his job and beaten up by a younger man, old Davies has been rescued by Aston and brought to the room. There seems to be no reason for this kindness. The old man takes stock of the scattered contents and inquires about the other rooms in the house. When Aston replies, "They're out of commission," we find ourselves in familiar Pinter country. Aston invites the old man to sleep with him in the room, until he gets "fixed up"; he gives him money and a key, lets him try on some old shoes.

After a night's sleep, the conversation is more erratic. When asked where he was born, the old man replies, "I was . . . uh . . . oh, it's a bit hard, like, to set your mind back . . . see what I mean . . . going back . . . a good way . . . lose a bit of track, like . . . you know. . . ." When Aston leaves, the old man examines the various objects in the room. Mick enters, watches silently, then suddenly springs and forces the old man to the floor. "What's the game?" he rasps at the old man, as Act I ends.

In Act II, Mick insistently questions the old man about his name, while the old man whines to Mick, "I don't know who you are!" Mick compares the old man to various outlandish relatives and acquaintances, refusing to believe the story of how he came to this room, of which he announces himself the owner, and his brother Aston the tenant. After Mick makes a long, caustic speech about the rent he intends to collect from the old man, Aston reenters. When Mick leaves the room Aston mentions his do-it-yourself remodeling plans for the house. Abruptly, Aston suggests that the old man become caretaker of the premises, but the old man thinks his assumed name may create difficulties.

When the old man next enters the room, it is dark, and he defends himself from an invisible enemy who proves to be Mick with an "electrolux." Friendly now, Mick confides to the old man that he cannot get Aston, his elder brother, to redecorate the premises. As owner, Mick offers the old man a job as caretaker. This time the old man quickly accepts, but Mick mentions the necessity for references. Reassuringly, the old man explains it is merely a question of getting down to Sidcup for his papers. If only he had a pair of shoes . . .

After a quick blackout, Aston wakens the old man so that he can start early for Sidcup, but the old man pleads that the weather is too bad. Aston closes Act II with a long monologue about his experiences in a mental hospital.

By Act III, the old man falls in with the wildly ambitious redecorating schemes of Mick. Since they have been living in the same room, Aston and the old man are mutual sources of irritation to each other. Feeling secure in his relationship with Mick, the old man carps at Aston's idiosyncrasies. When Aston suggests the old man find another place, he retorts, "You! You better find somewhere else." After the old man threatens Aston with a knife, the elder brother orders, "Get your stuff." Mumbling that Mick will protect him, the old man leaves temporarily.

But Mick turns on the old man, for Aston is his brother. Only if the old man is an interior decorator of great capability, can he stay. When the old man protests he is merely a caretaker, Mick accuses him of lying all the time, boasting about non-existent accomplishments. In the future, Mick intends to leave the house entirely in Aston's hands. "What about me?" pleads the old man. There is no answer as Aston enters and Mick leaves; when they pass each other, the two brothers smile briefly.

The old man attempts to make peace with Aston, and suggests various compromises to facilitate their living together, but to all of them Aston replies, "No." He does not need the old man's help, and will not have him as caretaker. More and more desperate, the old man begs to stay, but Aston turns his back on him. As the old man swears that he will go down to Sidcup for his papers so that he will have the proper references to be caretaker, "Aston remains still, his back to him, at the window," and the curtain falls on a "long silence" during which Aston is *as stone*.

Although Mick is slang for Irish, it is not clear in *The Caretaker* that Pinter is again designating the Christian tradition by an Irish name. Rather, the two brothers jointly seem to symbolize the family compatibility between a religious heritage and contemporary values. Thus, it is the elder, conventionally dressed Aston who is a carpenter, with its evocation of Christ, and it is the leather-jacketed Mick who is in the building trade and owns a motorized van. It is Mick who destroys a statue of Buddha, and who has grandiose schemes for redecorating the house. Aston's projects are humbler;

he has been restored to competence by modern treatments for mental deviates; before the end of the play, he does manage to tar the roof of the room, so it no longer leaks. Although Mick is presumably the owner and Aston the inhabitant of the house, the possession is finally left in doubt. As Mick explains, "So what it is, it's a fine legal point, that's what it is."

In their attitudes towards the old man, the human derelict, the two brothers present only surface contrasts. Mick begins by knocking him down, whereas Aston, instead of allowing him to die in despair, rescues him, shares his room with him, and opens up hope to him. Both the brothers name the old man as caretaker, offer him a kind of security, which they both subsequently withdraw. Mick turns his back on the old man for failing to fulfill a role to which he never aspired, but Aston rejects him for what he is—cantankerous, self-deluded, and desperate.

Of all Pinter's plays, *The Caretaker* makes the most bitter commentary on the human condition; instead of allowing an old man to die beaten, the System insists on tantalizing him with faint hope, thereby immeasurably increasing his final desperate anguish. There is perhaps a pun contained in the title: the Caretaker is twisted into a taker on of care, for care is the human destiny.

Pinter's drama savagely indicts a System which sports maudlin physical comforts, vulgar brand names, and vicious vestiges of a religious tradition. Pinter's villains descend from motorized vans to close in on their victims in stuffy, shabby rooms. The System they represent is as stuffy and shabby; one cannot, as in Osborne's realistic dramas, marry into it, or sneak into it, or even rave against it in self-expressive anger. The essence of the Pinter victim is his final sputtering helplessness.

Although Pinter's God-surrogates are as invisible as Godot, there is no ambiguity about their message. They send henchmen not to bless but to curse, not to redeem but to annihilate. As compared to the long, dull wait for Godot, Pinter's victims are more swiftly stricken with a deadly weapon—the most brilliant and brutal stylization of contemporary cliché on the English stage today.

Harold Pinter: *The Caretaker* and Other Plays

by James T. Boulton

> Subtle . . . experiences are for the most part incommunicable and indescribable, though social conventions or the terror of the loneliness of the human situation may make us pretend to the contrary.
>
> —I. A. Richards[1]

Naturalistic dramatists or dramatists wishing to present a rational argument would not subscribe to Richards' pronouncement. Shaw or Arnold Wesker presume that one human individual understands another, that logical exchange of ideas is the normal mode of communication, and that human actions are capable of explanation. Wesker and Shaw, for example, assume that they fully comprehend the motives of Sarah Kahn or Major Barbara and can demonstrate, by cause and effect, why these characters act as they do; they assume in other words that there is a logic of action and of thought and that both are capable of dramatic exposition. Further, such dramatists believe it important to make clear to their audience the stages in the logic of thought or action; in fact, this process goes part of the way to prove the validity of the thesis advanced by their plays. And even where the dramatist is not proposing a precise thesis, these comments still apply. John Osborne does not set out to "prove" anything in *Look Back in Anger,* but he considers it essential to provide evidence, for example, of Jimmy Porter's previous experience

"Harold Pinter: *The Caretaker* and Other Plays" by James T. Boulton. From *Modern Drama,* 6 (September 1963), 131–40. Reprinted by permission of the author and *Modern Drama.*

[1] *Principles of Literary Criticism* (1926), p. 33.

of suffering, his attitudes to the "Establishment," or his University education; the play, so to speak, advances from the point achieved by such evidence. There is a basic assumption that, given such-and-such information, a dramatist can document comparatively fully the subsequent actions and responses of his created figures.

Harold Pinter does not make such assumptions. He is concerned with "subtle experiences" but he sets out to evoke rather than exhaustively to depict or narrate them; by suggestion, hints, variations in intensity of mood, and the like, he involves the audience in an imaginative comprehension of the dramatic situation, the seeming triviality of which masks its deeper significance. One is reminded of Edwin Muir's comment on Kafka:

> In his diary he notes that when he tries to write on a set theme he is quite at a loss, but that as soon as he scribbles down a sentence such as "He stood at the window and looked down the street," he knows he is absolutely right. It is one of the quite ordinary doors through which he can enter the universal situation. Emerson says, "The way to the centre is everywhere equally short." [2]

Pinter appears to take a similar route and the more he writes the greater facility he develops to enter a universal situation. He does not set out to provoke sociological thinking or to address his audience on "Life" like Wesker or Osborne; rather he requires an imaginative response to the truth of human experience presented (with varying degrees of success) in his plays, and he thereby increases our range of sympathetic insight into the business of being human. And although Pinter denies that he uses symbols in any conscious way, his plays, though not fully allegorical, must be "interpreted" as poetic rather than prose drama. Evocative or disturbing speech, language which is an accurate reflection of colloquial English and yet reflects the mystery that Pinter sees as an inevitable feature of human relationships: this is the starting point for a consideration of his vision. It leads directly to what is perhaps the chief irony in his plays: the discrepancy between the implicit claim in any *patois* that it is the currency accepted and understood by all its users, and the dramatic fact that such language in actual usage reveals not complete communication between man and man but their essential apartness. "Every word you speak is open to any number of different

[2] *Essays on Literature and Society* (1949), p. 120.

interpretations" (Mick in *The Caretaker*),[3] "We all wander on our tod through this world. It's a lonely pillow to kip on" (Goldberg in *The Birthday Party*):[4] these quotations point to the central themes in Pinter's dramatic work.

"The terror of the loneliness of the human situation" is insisted upon time and again by Pinter. One means of demonstrating this fact is to show how he makes dramatic material out of the nostalgia for the supposed security to be found in the past, especially a childhood past, which appears to be endemic in our society. (The spate of biographies and autobiographies since the war, the popularity of television programmes which explore the early careers of famous contemporaries, the use of the bear and squirrel by Jimmy and Alison in *Look Back in Anger*—all such evidence indicates a common response to the modern predicament.) Pinter's characters frequently take refuge in nostalgic moods or attitudes, with the result that their insecurity and fearful loneliness are emphasized the more. In the opening speech in *The Room* Rose tries to offset her fear of losing the security represented by her single shabby room, by playing the role of mother to her silent husband, Bert:

> I don't know whether you ought to go out. I mean, you shouldn't, straight after you've been laid up. Still. Don't worry, Bert. You go. You won't be long.
> *She rocks*
> It's good you were up here, I can tell you. It's good you weren't down there, in the basement. . . .
> I'd have pulled you through. . . .
> [The weather] looks a bit better. It's not so windy. You'd better put on your thick jersey.
> *She goes to the rocking-chair, sits and rocks.*[5]

Later she helps him into his jersey, fetches his muffler and fixes it for him, and assures him cocoa will be ready for him on his return. The whole scene, linguistically and visually, suggests a mother-son relationship rather than wife-husband. The pathos springs from the sense of loneliness: Bert is isolated by his silence, Rose is herself isolated within the emotional world of her own creation. When Riley, the blind Negro, appears at the end of the play to threaten

[3] (1960), p. 77.
[4] *The Birthday Party and Other Plays* (1960), p. 59.
[5] In *The Birthday Party and Other Plays*, pp. 96–98.

this world with the message purporting to be from her father and requesting her return "home," Rose spurns him with an almost frenzied determination. We see Rose passionately trying to safeguard the world she has built up to hide her solitariness; her passion is translated into terms of physical violence by Bert, who recognises the threat represented by the intruding Negro; and the blindness transferred from Riley to Rose further emphasises her isolation which is now complete. She has rejected the demands made on her by family affection (whether we regard this as her own particular family or the larger human family of society); to respond to such demands would require active involvement in the affairs of others; Rose prefers to take refuge behind the flimsy emotional barrier she has laboriously erected against the outside world.

The Birthday Party (completed like *The Room* in 1957) exploits even further the nostalgia for the security of childhood. The landlady, Meg, has a possessive attachment for Stanley and she seems, in her unpleasantly sensual and flirtatious way, to act as a kind of mother-figure towards him; he, needing the protection such a relationship offers—"I don't know what I'd do without you," he says (p. 18)—responds in an equally distasteful manner. In fact, in the opening scene Pinter presents almost a parody, certainly a seedy version of a mother-son relationship.

> *Meg* [to her husband, Peter]. I made him [drink his tea]. I stood there till he did. I tried to get him up then. But he wouldn't, the little monkey. I'm going to call him. (*She goes to the door.*) Stan! Stanny! (*She listens.*) Stan! I'm coming up to fetch you if you don't come down! I'm coming up! I'm going to count three! One! Two! Three! I'm coming to get you! (p. 14)

The parody reaches its climax, after the arrival of the sinister figures Goldberg and McCann, with Meg's birthday present to Stanley—"a boy's drum." He beats it savagely in his fear of the two men who threaten to destroy his tenuous security. During the birthday party the conversation turns to childhood reminiscences and the significance of the drum becomes more apparent.

> *Meg.* There was a night light in my room, when I was a little girl. . . . And my Nanny used to sit up with me, and sing songs to me. . . . My little room was pink. I had a pink carpet and pink curtains, and I had musical boxes all over the room. And they played me to sleep. . . . (p. 63)

Meg is wellnigh drunk by this time, but her speech indicates the kind of relationship she had tried to establish with Stanley: in her emotional immaturity she has offered the security of a childhood world that has gone to seed. In the final act when Goldberg is recounting his visit to the bedroom of Lulu, the cheap boardinghouse prostitute, he remarks: "We sang a few of the old ballads and then she went to bye-byes." (p. 77) The leer sufficiently conveys the *double entendre* and brings the childish world of "bye-byes" into juxtaposition with the vicious adult world. And later even Goldberg, the gunman, in a state of nervous exhaustion, relies on snatches of childhood memories to establish some mental coherence. Men seem inevitably to turn away from a hostile and evil environment to the only degree of innocence they have ever known. And if one is reminded of the comment by Pinkie in Graham Greene's *Brighton Rock*—

> you had to go back a long way farther before you got innocence; innocence was a slobbering mouth, a toothless gum pulling at the teats, perhaps not even that; innocence was the ugly cry of birth.

the reminder may not be inappropriate.

There is much about this play—its seediness, professional thugs, a traitor on the run—which recalls the world of Graham Greene's novels. Particularly, one recalls Pinkie and his recourse to childhood memories when he is in a tight corner, but the fact that his memories are chiefly associated with religious experience makes one aware by contrast that Pinter's characters live in an ideological void. Their childhood is important because it represents a kind of cosy emotionalism within which they try vainly to shelter in escape from a present world of brutality; moreover, unlike Pinkie, it is their only (and a very precarious) hold on any sort of coherent and meaningful way of life. Once this hold is shattered or its precariousness fully revealed, breakdown follows: Rose's blindness or Stanley's nervous collapse in terror at Goldberg and McCann merely objectify this.

The settings Pinter chooses for his plays reinforce the feeling that his characters fear their isolation, strenuously look for security and cling to what shreds of it they have got, and are terrified at the intrusion of others into the private world they have created for themselves. A painting by Henry More—*Figures in a Setting* (1942)

—comes to mind in this context. A mother and child, and two other figures are depicted inside some sort of fortified building, and the impression given is of a fearful humanity secure so long as it remains inside the fortification but having no communication with the world outside. Pinter's vision is somewhat similar except that his characters feel little confidence in their flimsy security. The key visual symbol is, of course, the room which appears in the title of his first play: there, as Rose says, "You know where you are"; it is easily accessible as soon as she leaves the outside world—"It's not far up when you come in from outside"; and "nobody bothers us." (pp. 96, 97) When she is inside with her husband, she not only knows where she is but who she is; whenever anyone does bother her she is immediately suspicious and afraid. In *The Birthday Party* Stanley rarely, if ever, goes out of the boardinghouse, and in *The Dumb Waiter* the two hired killers, Ben and Gus, have no significance except within doors. They are never outside in daylight; they "can't move out of the house in case a call comes"; and when the outside world makes its presence felt either by means of an envelope containing matches pushed under the door of their basement room, or through the dumb waiter with its messages from a mysterious person above, the effect is always sinister and threatening. Although this play lacks the stature of the others mentioned so far—it has the air of a dramatised anecdote—there can be no doubt that Pinter creates a menacing atmosphere.

The language in which Pinter's vision is conveyed is fragmented and staccato; long speeches are rare and even when they occur they consist of brief sentences; indeed the language is appropriate to characters whose sense of security extends no further than the length of a few words. A Pinter character rarely indulges in abstract speculation: he is not of the same world as Wesker's Beatie Bryant (in *Roots*). His speech invariably remains close to the facts of experience whether that experience is "real" or imaginary, manufactured for the sake of impressing his hearers, elevating his status, or merely extricating himself from an awkward situation. Indeed, one of the fascinations of Pinter's dialogue is its psychological accuracy in the sense that, as in everyday life, the distinction between the truth which depends on verifiable fact and the truth to the speaker's vision of his own significance (which may involve anything from deliberate fabrication to mere exaggeration) is often blurred. And it is at these moments that an audience will find itself caught between laughter and serious acceptance. To take one sample: Stanley is speaking to McCann in Act II of *The Birthday Party,* realising that, with Goldberg, his listener is intent on avenging some unspecified crime.

> You know what? To look at me, I bet you wouldn't think I'd led such a quiet life. The lines on my face, eh? It's the drink. Been drinking a bit down here. But what I mean is . . . you know how it is . . . away from your own . . . all wrong, of course . . . I'll be all right when I get back . . . but what I mean is, the way some people look at me you'd think I was a different person. I suppose I have changed, but I'm still the same man that I always was. I mean, you wouldn't think, to look at me, really . . . I mean, not really, that I was the sort of bloke to—to cause any trouble, would you? (McCann *looks at him.*) Do you know what I mean?
>
> *McCann.* No. (p. 43)

The idiom is that of casual conversation; Stanley's mounting fear and his pleading tone of voice are authentically suggested by the changes of speed with which the speech is delivered: and his confusion increases the longer he is allowed to go on unchecked by his hearer. This is a man scared of the sound of his own voice; the longer he speaks the more he betrays his essential weakness by his repetitions, hesitancy, and irrelevance. But this irrelevance is dramatically valuable: we are convinced that Stanley is "the same man that [he] always was," that he cannot clearly distinguish between important qualities (loyalty and courage) and those which were dangerous perhaps to an I.R.A. man, and that, ironically, *because* he has not changed he has to be punished. Yet such an explanation leaves out of account our uncertainty as to how much of the speech refers to actual experience and genuine motives, and how much is being fabricated as Stanley goes along. The audience may find themselves on the edge of laughter, particularly at McCann's curt monosyllable which reminds one of the technique of a stage-comedian, but they are also uncomfortably aware that they are watching the movements of a mind prompted by terror and snivelling pride. Or again, Stanley's phrase "away from your own" is in itself a feeble cliché, but there is a level on which it is valid: Stanley has deserted his past and it may be that Goldberg and McCann's purpose is forcibly to take him back to "his own." Consequently, weaving their way through this apparently casual speech are elements that suggest both triviality and profound implications.

Only infrequently does communication break down completely, but Pinter's characters hang on to logic at the best of times only by the skin of their teeth. Logic after all presupposes that "b" follows "a" and then that inevitably "c" follows next; there is a confident expectation of continuous succession and development. The characters in these plays, however, lack this confidence except to a very limited degree. When logic breaks down, as it does in *The Room,* for example, during Rose's two exchanges with the landlord Mr. Kidd, and both speakers ignore what the other is saying, then for a moment we glimpse a world where communication is at an end and the chaos which is never far below the surface has become actual.

Pinter's fascination with human isolation and insecurity, his awareness of a brutal world where mystery and tension are always suddenly liable to appear, his recognition of the humor as well as the sinister which are part of human experience, and his control of his verbal medium—all these features reappear in his latest full-length play, *The Caretaker* (first presented in England 1960). This is undoubtedly his best play.

To begin with, in this play Pinter does not limit the significance of the action by linking the characters with any specific organisation such as the I.R.A., nor does he emphasize violence to the extent that it appears centrally important in human life as it did in *The Birthday Party* or *The Dumb Waiter,* nor again does he rely on gimmicks as at the end of the last-named play and to some extent in the finale of *The Room.* Violence has not completely disappeared from *The Caretaker* though on the stage its role is minimal; Davies' fear of violence, however, and his experience of it before the play opens, remind us of its continuing significance. What Pinter does in this play is—to quote Edwin Muir's words about Kafka—to open "one of the quite ordinary doors through which he can enter the universal situation": by selecting a tramp as his main character he introduces the archetypal symbol of life as a journey. It is not introduced with the formality of Beckett in *Waiting for Godot,* where one is always aware of its presence; rather the symbol is unobtrusively established by Davies' frequent references to his journeying "on the road" and his repeated requests for shoes—"I can't get anywhere without a pair of good shoes" (p. 54). Furthermore, the symbol is associated with something of the irony that is found in Beckett's play: life may be a journey but for present-day humanity it has no certain destination and there is little compulsion purposefully to undertake it. Davies talks often about his desire to be on the move again, particularly does he mention the man he wants to visit in Sidcup and for this purpose asks for shoes, but at the end of the play he is pleading not to be turned out to follow the road. "What am I going to do? What shall I do? Where am I going to go?" If life is a journey then not only is it along an uncertain road, it is also friendless and to some extent terrifying.

In this play, too, there is a much more even balance of sympathy evoked for the characters. In *The Room* and *The Birthday Party* we are principally involved with Rose and Stanley rather than with the people who threaten their security; here in *The Caretaker* while our sympathy is invited for Aston whose security is menaced, we are also involved on behalf of Davies as he loses his temporary refuge even though it is made plain that he is a destructive agent. The themes of human isolation and the search for security remain; the visual symbol of the room is still present; but the area of human sympathy has been extended. For there is fear and menace on both sides. Davies is frightened of the outside world; "them Blacks" (in reference to the Indian neighbours) becomes his explanation of any malign influence or event outside the walls of the room. His account of a begging visit to a monastery, absurd in its exaggeration, cannot be accepted as an accurate account of actual experience—nor perhaps does he expect Aston to take it as such; it is an account by a man who is seeking sympathy for his fear of a hostile world and for his reluctance to trust himself to it. Then there are the silent comings and goings of the brother Mick, the tricks played on Davies to reduce him to abject terror, the alarm created in him by the dilapidated house, and the suspicion bred in him by experiences before his arrival there. And although there may be some tenuous security for Davies inside the house, there is no peace; he is always on his guard against the two brothers. Indeed we are frequently reminded of "Big Brother." Davies, unknown to Aston, watches him while pretending to be asleep:

> He don't know I can see him, he thinks I'm asleep, but I got my eye on him all the time through that blanket, see? But he don't know that! He just looks at me and smiles, but he don't know that I can see him doing it! (p. 66)

The situation is amusing, but the implication is menacing. Furthermore Davies tries unsuccessfully to frighten Aston with the feeling that Mick is constantly watching him: "your brother's got his eye on you. He knows all about you. . . . Your brother's got his sights on you, man." (p. 71) Davies is in fact the outsider not only in the social sense, as a tramp, but also with regard to the relationship between the two brothers, Mick and Aston. Despite their lack of communication there is a bond of sympathetic understanding between them; they are the unified centre of the play's action. This emerges, for example, in a brief exchange when Davies and Mick are discussing what improvements could be made to the house:

> *Davies.* Who would live there?
> *Mick.* I would. My brother and me.
> *Pause*
> *Davies.* What about me?
> *Mick.* (*quietly*) All this junk here, it's no good to anyone. . . . (p. 64)

Although the brothers have given refuge to Davies, he is never accepted by them; by unspoken rejections such as the one above he is made to feel his isolation. Mick is actively suspicious of him, and Aston, despite his apparent naiveté, is quietly determined to expel the threat to his own achieved existence.

For his part Davies is not content with refuge; he seeks preeminence. With the same inevitability that leads the children in William Golding's novel, *The Lord of the Flies,* to reveal their human depravity, Davies boasts, lies, plays off one brother against the other, threatens Aston with expulsion from his own house, and generally exploits the kindness shown to him. There is no doubt that if Aston is to retain the tenour of his existence Davies has to go. There are two lines early in the play:

> *Davies.* You getting to the root of the trouble, are you?
> *Aston.* I've got a suspicion. (p. 21)

On one level they refer to the electric plug that Aston is forever trying to mend; on another they foreshadow the play's denouement.

Or again, the issue of identity—"who you are"—is raised in a more telling way in *The Caretaker.* It was implicit in *The Room* with the mysterious message brought by the Negro calling in question Rose's origin; it was present in *The Birthday Party* where Stanley's plea that he is the same man as he always was raises the problem of his identity—is he the man known to Meg or the man Goldberg and McCann believe him to be? In *The Caretaker* the problem is brought to our attention more forcibly. Davies' identity is frequently the focus of interest. He is not the person he pretends to be to society since he is using an assumed name (Jenkins); as Jenkins, so far as society is officially concerned (through insurance cards and the like) he does not exist and has no social rights; repeatedly he mentions the man at Sidcup who has papers—"They prove who I am" (p. 19)—but he makes no attempt to contact him and there is reason to doubt his existence; indeed Mick's remark, "You're a bloody impostor, mate!" (p. 76) seems to be both a statement of fact and a moral judgment. The identity of the brothers is not much clearer. One owns the house (but lives "somewhere else") and the other lives in it; Mick is a spiv who has a remarkable flow of language but whose activities remain mysterious, while Aston, after a spell in a mental hospital, finds difficulty in making sense of the world though he has some native shrewdness; one has elaborate plans for converting the house into flats but the ideas are daydreams never to be realised, while the other has dreams about doing something with his hands which will never materialise. When, therefore, Davies challenges Mick, "I don't know who you are," (p. 33) he is doing more than expressing ignorance of Mick's name.

The audience is in fact faced with a world of Kafka-like uncertainty; it is confronted with the question of identity at every turn. Pinter seems to suggest that man is a mystery, unknowable and yet fascinating, living in his own separate world which impinges only by accident on others equally separate, and it is these moments of impact that provide insight into the overall human situation. Cumulatively these insights add up to a view of man as moving further and further from a questionable innocence associated with childhood to the treacherous and evil world of experience; at once pathetic and humorous, man becomes a status-seeker looking for acceptance and security in a world that is unpredictable and has to be fought on its own terms; and because innocence has been lost, man cannot trust his fellows, does not frankly reveal himself to them, perhaps does not honestly know himself. But the insights are fragmentary and do not provide a definitive picture; therefore Pinter makes no concessions to the sort of objector whom Robert Browning answered (in a letter to Ruskin):

> You would have me paint it all plain out, which can't be; but by various artifices I try to make shift with touches and bits of outlines which *succeed* if they bear the conception from me to you.[6]

Pinter refuses to "paint it all plain out" because that would be to falsify his vision; he rejects naturalistic completeness of detail because his insights are not validated or limited by such considerations; rather he presents details which are also images requiring of the audience an act of imaginative comprehension.

[6] W. Collingwood, *Life of Ruskin* (1900), p. 164.

A Room and Some Views: Harold Pinter

by John Russell Taylor

"But what would you say your plays were *about*, Mr. Pinter?"
"The weasel under the cocktail cabinet."

—*exchange at a new writers' brains trust*

It is, in fact, tempting to see Pinter's progression from the earlier plays to the later in terms of a closer and closer approach to realism.[1] In the early plays the quiet, often wryly comic tone of the opening scenes is gradually replaced by something much more intense and horrific, and something considerably farther away from mundane considerations of likelihood. The probability of what happens, indeed, is never at issue: it is clear from the outset that this is a private world we have been permitted to enter, and as such, whatever relations with any outside world of objective reality we may imagine we perceive, it has its own consistency and carries its own conviction. In *The Room* neither the consistency nor the conviction is altogether unimpaired. The play was written in four days and sent off straight away with only minimum corrections to a friend at Bristol University. Unexpectedly, he offered to stage it, and so the text has become fixed in a form which Pinter now finds unsatisfactory. About the blind negro, the most evidently non-realistic character in his whole *œuvre,* he now says: "Well, it's very peculiar, when I got to that point in the play the man from the basement had to be introduced, and he just *was* a blind negro. I don't think

"A Room and Some Views: Harold Pinter." From John Russell Taylor, *Anger and After: A Guide to the New British Drama,* 2nd ed., rev. (London: Methuen & Co. Ltd., 1969). Reprinted by permission of Methuen & Co. Ltd., and A. D. Peters & Company.

[1] This essay is the central section of Mr. Taylor's survey of Pinter's work, a study that could not be included here in full.

there's anything radically wrong with the character in himself, but he behaves too differently from the other characters: if I were writing the play now I'd make him sit down, have a cup of tea. . . ." So in *The Birthday Party* the characters who embody the menace already behave much more normally—realistically, we might say—in their relations with Meg, with Lulu, the buxom blonde from down the road, and even with Stanley. Menace, the play implies, is a matter of situation: it does not come from extraordinary, sinister people, but from ordinary people like you and me; it is all a matter of circumstances whether at some point I suddenly become the menace in your life or you the menace in mine, and not anything inherent in either of us. Already Pinter is closer to reality than he was in dealing with the blind negro, and in *The Dumb Waiter* he comes closer still by elaborating the point about the normality of those who menace when they are outside the context in which their menace is exerted, and by leaving the violence implied in the final tableau instead of having it directly enacted on the stage. From here it is a short step to *A Slight Ache,* in which the nominal menace is completely passive and the real disruptive force exists in the mind of the menaced. There is no violence here at all, because no violence is needed.

The point at which this gradual change seems to crystallize in a single decision is in *The Caretaker,* where again we have the room, but no outside menace, simply a clash of personalities on the inside, and again we have to have one of the inhabitants displaced by another. Pinter has described his decision on how this should be done as follows:

> At the end . . . there are two people alone in a room, and one of them must go in such a way as to produce a sense of complete separation and finality. I thought originally that the play must end with the violent death of one at the hands of the other. But then I realized, when I got to the point, that the characters as they had grown could never act in this way. . . .

In other words, here for the first time psychological realism overtly won out; these, as much as the inhabitants of "The Black and White," are people existing, making their own decisions, creating the circumstances of their own lives, and not in any sense the puppets of fate, as were in many respects the characters of *The Room, The*

Birthday Party, and *The Dumb Waiter. The Caretaker* still works completely in terms of a private myth, as they did, but it gains in richness and complexity by also working completely, as they did not, on the quite different level at which comprehensible motivation comes into play: for the first time we can sensibly consider (if we want to) why the characters do what they do as well as, more obscurely, why what happens has the effect it does on us.

There are three characters: two brothers, Mick and Aston, and an old tramp, Davies, whom Aston has invited back to his room. Aston is strangely laconic and withdrawn, and it eventually emerges that he was in a mental home two years before and received electrical shock treatment which has left him as he is. His brother is trying to get through to him, to arouse his interest in something, and Aston had been collecting materials for some time with the intention of building a shed, but shows little sign of getting down to it. Davies, in fact, is the first thing in which he has shown positive interest since the mental home; he likes him and likes his company. Mick's jealousy is instantly aroused, and his one thought is to get the old man out, but he can do this satisfactorily from his own point of view only if Aston voluntarily rejects Davies. So, hiding his dislike behind a mask of flippancy Davies takes for good humour, Mick confides his plans to Davies and leads him on to suppose that he is quite amiably disposed and will hire him as caretaker for the house when it is fitted up. Davies falls into the trap by trying to play one brother against the other, rejecting Aston, his real friend, and throwing in his lot with Mick. He even goes so far as to curry favour with Mick by saying that Aston is mad, and then Mick has him where he wants him:

> What a strange man you are. Aren't you? You're really strange. Ever since you come into this house there's been nothing but trouble. Honest, I can take nothing you say at face value. Every word you speak is open to any number of different interpretations. Most of what you say is lies. You're violent, you're erratic, you're just completely unpredictable. You're nothing else but a wild animal, when you come down to it, you're a barbarian. And to put the old tin lid on it, you stink from arse-hole to breakfast-time. Look at it. You come here recommending yourself as an interior decorator, whereupon I take you on, and what happens? You make a long speech about all the references you've got down at Sidcup, and what happens? I

haven't noticed you go down to Sidcup to obtain them. It's all most regrettable, but it looks as though I'm compelled to pay you off your caretaking work. Here's half a dollar.

Rejected by Mick, Davies tries desperately to make it up with Aston, but it is too late, and he has gone too far: Aston has determined to start work on his shed ("If I don't get it up now it'll never go up. Until it's up I can't get started."), and there is no place in his life for Davies, who has no alternative before him as the curtain falls but to leave.

As the speech just quoted suggests, the style of *The Caretaker* is much more direct than that of Pinter's earlier plays. Everything that Aston says—suitably enough, considering his mental condition—is perfectly clear and unequivocal. And though Mick's mental processes are devious the intention behind everything he says is clear, even when he is talking apparently at random just to unsettle the old man (there are several examples of this in the second act—the long irrelevant comparisons with his uncle and the bloke he knew in Shoreditch, the fantastic excursion in which he pretends to be letting the flat to Davies). Only Davies is subject in his conversation to the characteristic Pinter ambiguity, and this is here symptomatic not of the general unknowability of things, but of a specific intention on the character's part to cover his tracks and keep people guessing about himself. Not that there isn't a certain forlorn conviction in his assertions that everything would be right if only he could get down to Sidcup and collect his papers, but evidently this is a story he has told so often to excuse himself that now he himself half believes it—whether there is any truth in it at all we have no way of knowing. Whenever he is asked a direct question he either evades answering it directly (when asked if he is Welsh he replies, after a pause, "Well, I been around, you know") or by offering an apparently unequivocal answer which ten minutes later he will contradict with another equally unequivocal statement.

Shortly before *The Caretaker* was produced Pinter provided a gloss on his use of this sort of contradiction and ambiguity in a programme note to the Royal Court production of *The Room* and *The Dumb Waiter*.

The desire for verification is understandable, but cannot always be satisfied. There are no hard distinctions between what is real and

> what is unreal, nor between what is true and what false. The thing is not necessarily either true or false; it can be both true and false. The assumption that to verify what has happened and what is happening presents few problems, I take to be inaccurate. A character on the stage who can present no convincing argument or information as to his past experiences, his present behaviour or his aspirations, nor give a comprehensive analysis of his motives is as legitimate and as worthy of attention as one who, alarmingly, can do all these things. The more acute the experience the less articulate its expression.

But as a moment's consideration shows, this applies much more readily to Pinter's earlier works than to those he was at that time writing. In *The Caretaker* verification is seldom a problem. If we want to know why Aston is as he is, he tells us in detail at the end of the second act, and no doubt is ever cast on what he says. If we want to know exactly what Mick's game is, there is enough clear indication throughout, and even though his way of reaching his goal is rather indirect—necessarily if he is to edge the cunning old tramp out and at the same time make sure that Aston also wants him to leave—by the last act the intention underlying all he does becomes unmistakable. Only with Davies is there any difficulty about verification: we have no way of knowing whether he has really left any papers at Sidcup, what really happened at the monastery where he hoped to be given a pair of shoes (if it existed and if he ever went there), or which of the other recollections which scatter his conversation are true or false. But even here the desire for verification is nowhere near the forefront of our minds, because none of this, even by normal standards of play-making, is vital to our understanding (in the way that, for instance, we would normally require to know precisely what Stanley had done to bring judgement on him in *The Birthday Party*, who the blind negro in *The Room* was, who Edward in *A Slight Ache* thinks the match-seller might be). All we need to understand about Davies for the purposes of the play is that he is shifty, unreliable, and probably incapable of telling the truth even if he wanted: his evasions and contradictions imply a judgement on him, but not necessarily on the world around him.

In fact, the play seems to be built upon a proposition new in Pinter's work, one which he has expressed as "simple truth can often be something much more terrifying than ambiguity and doubt." The classic instance of this is Aston's speech at the end of Act 2, when he explains about his experiences before, during, and after his treatment at the mental home. As first performed, this seemed quite out of context, being made into a direct, self-pitying appeal for sentimental sympathy, a thin patch representing a weak point in the intricately woven texture of the whole work. But when one studies the play in print it becomes obvious that it is, in fact, no such radical departure from the style of the rest of the play; Aston, indeed, never speaks—could never speak—in any other style, and there is no basic ambiguity in the play in relation to which this single major deviation into unequivocal sense would be artistically impossible. If the monologue were played, as the rest of the text demands it be played, impersonally, almost entirely without expression, as though the speaker were under hypnosis or describing something which happened to someone else, it would become legitimately the climax of horror in the play, the inevitable moment of reckoning with the past—Stanley's ordeal, in effect, but this time self-inflicted, and therefore something from which Aston can begin to recover in the third act by resolving anew really to get started on his shed.

This new directness and simplicity is to be found also in the television-cum-radio play Pinter was writing immediately before, *A Night Out,* and his next television play *Night School.* In *A Night Out* the protagonist, Albert, suffers from the attentions of a clinging, possessive mother, and the play chronicles his attempts to escape from her for one evening. First there is a firm's party he has to go to and which his mother blandly refuses to take into account by disregarding everything he says on the subject. When he finally shakes her off and goes everything goes wrong, the whole thing culminating in a "liberty" taken by the old employee in whose honour the party is given with a young woman, for which Albert is blamed. He leaves, and on his return has to suffer a long, self-pitying monologue from his mother embodying a series of variations on her favourite theme, that if he wants to go out and leave her he must be leading an unclean life, "mucking about with girls" or frequenting low pubs.

The end of the second act leaves him, the worm turned at last, poised with a clock above his head as though about to attack her, and exactly what has happened remains in doubt until the end of the third. When we next encounter Albert he is succumbing to the advances of a terribly genteel prostitute, with whom he exchanges fantasies: he is an assistant director in films, she a respectable mother with a daughter at a select boarding-school near Hereford. But finally, the suppressed violence in his mind coming to the surface, he threatens her, too, with a clock, obviously substituting her for his mother. ("Who do you think you are? You talk too much, you know that? You never stop talking. Just because you're a woman you can get away with it. . . . You're all the same, you see you're all the same, you're just a dead weight around my neck.") He shatters her dream about a daughter by demonstrating that the photograph is actually of her as a child, and then having exercised his power over her by making her put on and do up his shoes he leaves and returns home to a tearful, forgiving, and quite unharmed mother, ready to stifle him as much as ever with her neurotic solicitude. The night out is over.

Here again the question of verification and its problems does not arise; the motivation of all the characters is made quite clear, and even the one or two points on which some doubt exists are rapidly cleared up: the photograph in the prostitute's room is proved to be of herself by an inscription on the back, and the perpetrator of the "liberty," left in doubt in the radio version of the play, is unequivocally identified in the television version. (The script direction reads: "The camera closes on Mr. Ryan's hand, resting comfortably on his knee, and then to his face which, smiling vaguely, is inclined to the ceiling. It must be quite clear from the expression that it was his hand which strayed.") Instead, the play concerns itself with the working out of the relationship between Albert and his mother, and the impossibility of their communicating with one another, or at least the impossibility of his communicating with her. Albert is more intelligent than his mother, but he is weak, and so her stupidity makes her impregnable: she just cannot, or will not, understand anything which does not suit her, and when he goes against her wishes she regards this not as evidence that he is an adult with a mind of his own, but simply as the wilfulness of a child, to be rebuked but not taken too seriously. It is the Stanley-Meg situation over again, except that this time Albert has not chosen it and resents it; he has not discovered, as Stanley has, the way of turning his mother's stupidity to his own purpose, and all his gestures of rebellion are impotent. Though he insists on going to the party, once he has his way guilt overtakes him and he tries to get out of it by feigning illness; the party itself is bound to be disastrous for him because he has insisted on going against his mother's wishes. And even when he resorts to physical violence he cannot win: he has to be content with a substitute victory against a substitute victim, the prostitute to whom he pours out the reproaches about her endless talking and the matter of the light in Grandma's bedroom which should by rights be directed at his mother. The final insult, perhaps, his mother's willingness, after all this has happened, to forget everything and let things be just as they were before, since it is the final demonstration that Albert does not count and nothing he can do really matters.

A Night Out offers convincing proof, if proof were needed, that Pinter does not rely in his plays entirely on his ingenuity in thinking up situations of horror and mystery and then giving them a superficial reality by exploiting his undeniable skill at capturing in his dialogue the precise nuances of everyday speech. As in *The Caretaker,* the people in it make their situations rather than being created by them, and in so far as the situations in *A Night Out* are nearer the world in which most of us live than those in *The Caretaker,* we are better able to appreciate at once Pinter's success in the mode of psychological realism. And this, even though the integrity of his dramatic private world remains unimpaired: the myopically detailed, obsessive quality of his observation is just as much in evidence here as before and the effect is to charge a story which could be treated in a simple, conventionally "realistic" fashion (something one could hardly say of any of the earlier plays) with the sort of feverish intensity which Alain Robbe-Grillet at his best sometimes achieves. In fact, the play demonstrates again a basic fact in Pinter's work—that it often seems least realistic when it is closest to actuality. For the form of the dialogue, with its constant leapfrogging and casting-back in sense, its verbal misunderstandings, anticipations which prove to be mistaken, mishearings and all the other characteristics of everyday speech which most dramatists iron out into a logical, grammatical *lingua franca* which passes on the stage for realistic speech, recalls rather the sort of photopuzzles *Lilliput* used to publish in its heyday, in which details of familiar objects would be vastly enlarged so that the grains and textures stood out with hallucinary precision and all the normal associative connotations were stripped from them. In effect this is reality turned against itself, for showing something so closely, with such fanatical accuracy, makes it seem far less real and familiar than the conventional simplifications of our normal dilatory middle view.

Pinter's next television play, *Night School,* takes up again and develops certain themes from *A Night Out,* but their handling is rather arbitrary and Pinter later revised it for radio before publishing it, saying that it contains "characteristics that implied I was slipping into a formula. It so happens this was the worst thing I have written. The words and ideas had become automatic, redundant." Certainly the main thing to strike one about it in performance was the low level of intensity at which it worked: obviously intended to be a light comedy exploiting the new realistic vein in Pinter's work, it failed mainly because it seemed that the author had deliberately reduced the mechanical interest of his plot (all the ambiguities are resolved completely in a way which offers no surprises) in order to let his characters act and interact very much as they do in *The Caretaker* and *A Night Out,* but then failed to create characters interesting enough to hold our attention on this level.

A number of the old themes are recapitulated in various ways: the basic conflict of the play, for instance, is a battle for the possession of a room which represents for the protagonist, Walter, an unsuccessful forger just home from prison, quiet and security. ("If only I could get my room back! I could get settled in, I could think, about things.") Unfortunately in his absence his aunts have let it to an apparently genteel, respectable young woman who claims that she teaches in a night school. Again the minor ambiguities and contradictions are significant in terms of character rather than as implied comments on reality: Walter is a liar, but he lies to achieve his various purposes and the discrepancies between his various statements seem only to tell us more about him; the old scrap-dealer Solto is an inveterate boaster, but the truth or otherwise of his boasts never comes into question. In fact, the problem of verification resolves itself into one single question: is Sally, the supposed night-school teacher, what she seems, or is she really the night-club entertainer to whom she bears a quite inexplicable resemblance? And this question is answered for us, unsurprisingly, before the end; the two Sallys are, in fact, one, and when Walter seems to be getting too warm in his attempts to establish their identity she leaves.

The connection of all this with the last act of *A Night Out* is obvious: it might almost be a portrait of the girl there as seen through the eyes of the other occupants of the house where she lives (apparently respectable enough for her visitors to have to creep round in stockinged feet). A number of details are also carried over: the play with the photograph of Sally in a gym slip recalls the other girl's deception with a photograph of herself when young, and Walter's strange bout of obsessive ordergiving, when he makes Sally repeatedly cross and uncross her legs, recalls Albert's orders to the other girl—except that there the scene had its dramatic *raison d'être,* while here it seems merely arbitrary, arising from nothing we know of in Walter's character and serving no apparent purpose in the play as a whole except to give it a sensational highlight. The main point of interest about *Night School,* in fact, is its demonstration that Pinter can, like anyone else, make his mistakes, but that (*a*) he is the first to acknowledge them, and (*b*) even when his imagination is working at decidedly less than full throttle he still remains true to his world and produces something which, though markedly inferior to his best work, could still have been written by no one else.

If *Night School* implied that Pinter was "slipping into a formula," his next work, the radio play *The Dwarfs,* shows him triumphantly escaping the danger. It carried him off on a new line of inquiry which was to prove highly significant in his further development; it has certainly been his most difficult play yet and the most daunting to popular taste. As a matter of fact, its genesis dates back a number of years, to the long, unpublished novel of the same title Pinter wrote between 1953 and 1957. In that there were four main characters, three men and a girl, but in the play only the three men appear, Pete, Mark, and Len. Pete and Mark as we encounter them are "typical Pinter characters"; they indulge in dilatory, inconsequential conversations with each other and with Len, avoiding real communication as far as possible. Our clearest picture of them comes from Len, with his images of them: Pete, walking by the river, cruel and predatory like a gull, digging under a stone in the mud; Mark, sitting smooth and complacent by his fireside, like a spider in his web. But they are for us almost entirely projections of Len's consciousness; each is convinced that the other is bad for Len, that not Len but only he can manage the other, and this is almost all we know of them objectively: this, and that vanity is the dominant force in Mark's character—otherwise completely negative, he is stirred to action only when he learns from Len that Pete thinks he is a fool.

But Len is a very different case; we learn a lot more about him, and in a way that is completely new in Pinter's writing—we are actually allowed to enter his mind. We have never really known what went on in the minds of Pinter characters before, and the mystery of what they could possibly be thinking, the tension between the known and the unknown, was a large part of the earlier plays' fascination. In the later plays the characters become noticeably more scrutable; we can guess quite often what is in their minds but, except for Aston's speech in *The Caretaker,* we are never told. The freedom of radio has allowed Pinter in this play, however, to switch at will from ordinary conversation to a stream-of-consciousness monologue, and monologue, moreover, from a stream of consciousness far wider and deeper and more turbulent than Aston's, for while Aston is numbed as a result of his shock treatment at the mental home, Len still has that desperate remedy to come; he is hovering on the brink of insanity, and when we leave him is perhaps already in a mental home. (Or is he? It depends whether Pete is being evasive when he says that Len is in hospital suffering from "kidney trouble," or simply stating a fact.)

The creatures which bedevil Len's mind are the dwarfs, who are ever busy gobbling up garbage, organizing and arranging, observing Len, Pete, and Mark, until finally, mysteriously, they leave. Who are they? What are they? Well, who is anyone, come to that? This is the central theme of the play, summed up in Len's climactic speech to Mark:

> The point is, who are you? Not why or how, not even what. I can see what, perhaps, clearly enough. But who are you? It's no use saying you know who you are just because you tell me you can fit your particular key into a particular slot which will duly receive your particular key because that's not foolproof and certainly not conclusive. Just because you're inclined to make these statements of faith has nothing to do with me. It's not my business. Occasionally I believe I perceive a little of what you are, but that's pure accident. Pure accident on both our parts, the perceived and the perceiver. It's nothing like an accident, it's deliberate, it's a joint pretence. We depend on these accidents, on these contrived accidents, to continue. It's not im-

portant then that it's conspiracy or hallucination. What you are, or appear to be to me, or appear to be to you, changes so quickly, so horrifyingly, I certainly can't keep up with it and I'm damn sure you can't either. But who you are I can't even begin to recognize, and sometimes I recognize it so wholly, so forcibly, I can't look, and how can I be certain of what I see? You have no number. Where am I to look, where am I to look, what is there to locate, so as to have some surety, to have some rest from this whole bloody racket? You're the sum of so many reflections. How many reflections? Is that what you consist of? What scum does the tide leave? What happens to the scum? When does it happen? I've seen what happens. But I can't speak when I see it. I can only point a finger. I can't even do that. The scum is broken and sucked back. I don't see where it goes, I don't see when, what do I see, what have I seen? What have I seen, the scum or the essence? What about it? Does all this give you the right to stand there and tell me you know who you are? It's a bloody impertinence. . . .

Here a number of themes implicit in Pinter's previous works come to the surface and are defined in terms which show clearly the way his work is leading. Little by little the desire for verification has shifted from the audience into the play they are watching; instead of watching with a degree of mystification the manœuvres of a group of characters who seem perfectly to understand what they are doing but simply offer us no means of sharing that understanding, we are now required to watch understandingly the manœuvres of people who do not understand their situation but are trying laboriously to establish the truth about it. And this truth goes beyond the mere verification of single facts (except, perhaps, in the comedies) to a quest for the how and the why, the who and the what, at a deeper level than demonstrable fact. This involves a new preoccupation with the means of communication, since the question comes back, will people tell the truth about themselves, and if they will, can they? Everyone wants to know the truth about others without letting them know the truth about him—the feeling that once someone is called by his true name he is in the power of the caller lies deep. Pinter has said that his characters are "at the extreme edge of their living, where they are living pretty much alone." Even if the disposition to communicate at this level exists at all, is it a possibility? Reality itself is so complex, and changes so quickly, that our only hope is an unspoken conspiracy whereby we tacitly agree to accept certain formulas as true, some constant patterns beneath the constantly changing surface of things. A man may change alarmingly from moment to moment, but for the sake of argument we presume that there is one coherent being underneath; the tide may come and go, the scum be broken and sucked back, but behind the superficial restlessness and change lies the monumental consistency of the unchanging sea.

But is this so? In his next two plays, *The Collection* and *The Lover* (both originally written for television) Pinter sets out to explore the question further, within the context of relations between husband and wife. No longer is there any question of *failure* of communication; in both plays the characters are educated and articulate, they are capable of expressing to each other whatever they want to express. If they want to tell the truth about themselves they have at their disposal the means of doing so, but of course they don't want to, and it remains highly doubtful whether even if they did they could. What each wants to know about the other, and what we want to know about them, is essentially unknowable, perhaps does not even exist—it is the one face behind the faces. They want to break through "the joint pretence" upon which "we depend to continue," and discover the truth, even though "The thing is not necessarily either true or false; it can be both true and false." In other words, we are back with verification, but at a deeper level at which the desire to achieve it is inevitably and inescapably doomed to failure, since it is not a matter, even conceivably, of verifiable fact (as, say, the reasons for Stanley's persecution by Goldberg and McCann in *The Birthday Party* might be). In *The Collection* this does not immediately appear to be so: ostensibly the matter at issue is whether Stella and Bill, two young fashion designers at the same out-of-town show, did or did not sleep with each other. But when Stella's husband James sets out to meet and question Bill he does not seem to be looking for the truth about that. She has told him it happened, and apparently he believes her. No, the truth he wants to find is the truth about her; he will know more about her if he gets to know the man she has found attractive enough to go to bed with at first meeting. He doesn't, of course: the more contradictory accounts emerge, the more lies, equivocations, and halftruths pile up, the less anyone knows about anyone. The defensive mechanisms of human beings are too well-ordered for them to do anything else but go smoothly into action at the mere hint from an outsider that given half a chance he will find out the whole truth, pin one down, and categorize one forever.

When James sets out with sinister amiability to terrorize Bill (the menace of the earlier plays given background: to Bill, James is at first a nameless and inexplicable terror from outside, but we know why he is doing what he is doing), Bill begins by denying anything happened, then agrees and starts to elaborate. But there is another party interested, Harry, a suave, middle-aged art fancier, who as he tells us found Bill in the gutter and with whom Bill lives on terms of suspicious intimacy. While James is persuading Bill to corroborate Stella's story, Harry is persuading Stella to retract it and say that nothing really happened at Leeds at all. Harry arrives back just as James is getting threatening and indulging in a little knife-throwing (none too successfully; again, the menace is humanized) and when faced with Stella's new version of the incident Bill breaks down and agrees that in fact all that happened was that they sat in the hall for two hours talking about what they would do if they went to her room. It sounds like the truth, but when the play ends James has returned to the attack with Stella and is getting no satisfactory answer from her. . . .

The business of verification, of finding out "the truth," has become an elaborate manœuvre, a highly serious game like something in *Les Liaisons Dangereuses* (here, for instance, every possible combination of the principals is permitted except that of the two people, Bill and Stella, who were actually present on the occasion in question—if they *were* there, of course—and who alone could perhaps tell us what really happened), but in which what is to be decided may well be a matter of life and death. It is vitally important to James that he should find out what sort of woman Stella is, faced suddenly with the picture of an unknown woman who yet lives in the same body with his wife. Which is the real Stella? If he knows "the facts" for certain, will he be any nearer a solution? Can the game be played through to a decisive conclusion, or is it doomed to end in deadlock?

For James at any rate it is unlikely to bring satisfaction, because he is naive enough to demand the truth, but the couple in *The Lover* expect nothing so simple. They are, apparently, happily married, with the husband complacently asking his wife as he leaves the house for work if her lover is coming this afternoon and solicitously inquiring afterwards how it was. But when we finally see the lover we discover that he is the husband, differently dressed: it is some sort of elaborate game they play by which they separate the staid husband-wife relationship and the passionate lover-mistress relationship which together make up their marriage. Indeed, so well do they separate them that they begin to act as though they are in fact being unfaithful to each other, telling half-truths about their relationships and becoming jealous of their own *alter egos.* It is in a sense the situation of Osborne's *Under Plain Cover* again, only explored far more deeply: it is not just a game for keeping the marriage fresh and exciting, but an acceptance of the inescapable fact that each person is "the sum of so many reflections"—husband and lover, rapist and protector (within the lover-mistress situation there are further refinements in which they pretend to be first of all a woman in a park and a sinister stranger who makes menacing advances, then the same woman, prepared now to be provocative, and an apparently kindly park-keeper who intervenes on her behalf and then becomes the willing accomplice in her coquetry); sober, responsible wife, intelligent mistress, whore. . . . And it all amounts to a successfully working marriage of ten years' standing, with children (at boarding school) and no outside involvements. Any menace to the status quo comes entirely from within; if the arrangement looks like breaking down, it is only because the desire to have things clear and unequivocal is part of basic human nature and almost impossible to vanquish. However, Richard and Sarah appreciate the necessity of vanquishing it, the impossibility indeed of living together on any other terms except the acceptance of an infinitude of reflections in lieu of the unknowable, perhaps non-existent, essence. So perhaps if Max, Richard's lover-persona, can visit in the evening as well as the afternoon. . . .

The Lover represents to date Pinter's furthest exploration of human nature in its irrevocably fragmented form; his most whole-hearted acceptance of the idea first clearly formulated in *The Dwarfs* that the Fall of man is more like Humpty-Dumpty's than Adam's and Eve's, resulting in a situation where nobody, oneself or another, can hope to put all the pieces together again into a perfect and coherent whole. Significantly, the only people in Pinter's plays who appear to tell the whole truth, into whose minds indeed we are permitted to look, are madmen—one permanently mutilated in the course of his "cure," the other clearly tottering, when we meet him, on the brink of a complete breakdown. If Aston in *The Caretaker* allows himself to be wholly known it is only because, as he is now, there is little to know; and though Len in *The Dwarfs* speaks directly to us, as far as possible, by way of an internal monologue, the more we learn about him the less we really know him. Between *The Room* and *The Lover* we have in effect run the complete dramatic gamut from total objectivity to total subjectivity, and discovered in the process that there are no clear-cut explanations of anything. At one end of the scale no motives are explained and everything remains mysterious; at the other as many motives as possible are expounded for us, and if anything the result is more mystifying than before. It is only from a middle distance, as in *The Caretaker* and *A Night Out,* that we can see a picture simple enough to hold out the possibility that we may understand it, that we are given enough in the way of motive to reach some provisional conclusions on the characters and their actions. It is a perfect demonstration of the conspiracy on which normal human intercourse relies, and incidentally of the knife-edge on which dramatic "realism" rests: if we were told a little less about what is going on it would be incomprehensible, but if we were told a little more the difficulty of establishing any single coherent truth would be just as great.

Clearly, for all sorts of reasons, Pinter's drama could not stick at this comfortable middle distance: ever the most meticulously logical and consistent of dramatists in his development from one play to the next, he was impelled progressively to explore what Len in *The Dwarfs* called the "contrived accidents" of character-perception on which we depend to continue. But in the process it might seem that he was working himself into a logical and dramatic impasse. In a world where everybody is the sum of so many reflections, where nobody is the same even to himself (supposing that means anything) for two seconds together, and where nobody can be sure even of accurately perceiving what anyone else may be at any given moment, we depend on the joint pretence that people have some sort of underlying consistency, and that perceptions can at least to some extent be relied on, in order to continue living at all. And writing plays, for if the joint pretence is shattered, how shall the dramatist hope to shape or make sense of his material? Both *The Collection* and *The Lover* grapple with this problem, but in them any recognizable reality seems to be dissolving before our eyes. Even more was this the case with his next work, the television play *The Basement* (produced in 1967 but actually written three years earlier as a film script). This is a relatively slight work, the core of which—a man invites an old friend into his flat out of the rain, the guest brings in a girl and then proceeds to take over the flat and all the owner's possessions—is to be found in a short snatch of dramatic dialogue, *Kullus,* which Pinter wrote as long ago as 1949. The development of the situation, with its shifting of power and changing of role between the two men, is new, and the main interest of the piece is that it extends Pinter's preoccupation with the fragmented nature of experience beyond character to include physical surroundings as well, with the décor of the basement flat changing completely and unpredictably from shot to shot.

With the "joint pretence" so completely rejected, all coherent, consistent vision reduced to so many shattered reflections, one could not help wondering what could logically come next for Pinter the dramatist but silence? What did come next was the television play *Tea Party,* in which withdrawal from the extreme position of the plays which preceded it is actually dramatized. In *Tea Party,* Disson, the central character, an apparently very successful businessman, suffers anguish from perceiving the frailty of the joint pretence. Is his wife's brother in fact her lover, or both, or neither? Were they brought up where and how they say they were, or not, or both yes and no? We start with him, and up to a certain point in the play we see things through his eyes. But then we come gradually to appreciate that he is in fact going mad. If, in a game of ping-pong, he goes to hit two balls it is not necessarily because two, or an infinite number of balls are or may be coming at him, but simply that for more or less complex reasons connected with his own mental situation he sees two balls when in fact, "really," there is only one. That is, what we are seeing is not to be taken as an image of the world as it is, but simply as one man's increasingly demented view of it. The two viewpoints fight it out during the climactic tea-party, when Disson's view of it and our "objective" view are intercut, until finally the objective wins out and we are left decisively outside the character, in objective reality, looking on while he remains in a state of complete trance, unseeing, unhearing, paralysed (literally) by his own inability to make sense of the world around him. His situation at the end of the play might almost be symbolic of a dramatist's situation when he sees so many mutually exclusive possibilities coexistent in any character or situation that he has to stop even trying to fit them into one coherent dramatic pattern. This might well have been Pinter's situation after *The Basement,* but the end of *Tea Party,* significantly, takes us (and him) a stage further: the battle between objective and subjective viewpoints has been resolved in favour of the objective, and reality is reintegrated, leaving the unfortunate Disson as odd man out because he has contracted out of reality.

Pinter's Usurpers

by John Pesta

In barely a decade Harold Pinter has produced an impressive volume of work, insisting in play after play on the precariousness of man's existential security. Pinter's device for expressing this theme has been the "usurper," a menacing figure who, either actively or passively, undermines the existence of other characters, and who sometimes is himself undermined.

In early plays like *The Room, The Dumb Waiter,* and *The Birthday Party* this figure appears as a mysterious agent in direct conflict with a gradually disintegrating victim. Later works such as *The Caretaker, The Servant,* and *The Homecoming* explore more complicated relationships between the usurpers and their victims; the plays become subtle psychological studies of characters who are at once aggressive, yet in need of personal relationships to supply the security which they desperately require.

In Pinter's first play, *The Room,* a blind Negro, Riley, intrudes into the sanctuary which Bert, a man of fifty, and Rose, sixty, have shaped. The discrepancy in their ages is important since one aspect of their closely held security involves the motherliness with which Rose looks after Bert, and also because Rose will be summoned to die and the younger Bert will violently resist the summons. After an atmosphere of tension is developed through Rose's fears of the world outside the room and particularly of the stranger in the basement, this mysterious figure, Riley, appears with a message from Rose's "father" to "come home." Unwilling to leave, Rose first reacts hysterically, insulting Riley; gradually, however, she accedes to his request. She responds to Riley's "Come home now, Sal," by touching his eyes and head; at this instant, Bert re-enters. At sight of the

"Pinter's Usurpers" by John Pesta. From *Drama Survey,* 6 (Spring 1967), 54–65. Reprinted by permission of the author and *Drama Survey.*

tableau he draws the curtains, blotting out the dangerous outer world which is tempting Rose. His own mounting hysteria—many of Pinter's characters, like Kafka's, seem to exist on the edge of hysteria—is suggested by his rambling mutterings in which he reconstructs actions he has just performed outside; it is a pitiful attempt to reassure himself of the stability of his existence. He ends by murdering Riley, whose blindness is passed on to Rose.

The play calls for a symbolic interpretation. Riley, threatening the womblike security of the room, serves as a death figure. Bert's violence is futile, for while Riley dies, his stigma is passed on to Rose. The play's effect is hopeless and pathetic. The element of the supernatural in *The Room* has opened the play to serious criticism. Martin Esslin, for instance, objects to its "lapse from horror, built up from elements of the commonplace, into crude symbolism, cheap mystery, and violence." Riley's murder and Rose's blinding, are, according to Esslin, melodramatic devices which contradict the subtly built-up terrors of the opening scenes. Mystery has become threadbare mystification.[1]

This criticism is justified to some extent, for Pinter's first plays employ elements of the incredible which later plays dispense with in favor of more realistic situations. However, the situation in *The Room* seems more complex than is implied by the interpretation which sees Riley simply as the aggressive usurper and Rose and Bert as his co-victims. Riley does menace the security of the room, but his summons to Rose to "come home," even if it is the call of death, need not be regarded as an altogether fearful summons. It may be a call to leave a life of fearful security and gain a richer life of memory and freedom by acknowledging her past, or by accepting death—not that these are the same, but that they cover both the realistic and symbolic dimensions of the play; Rose's "father" at first seems a realistic, earthly figure, and later takes on the character of a symbol for the divine. "Going home" has traditionally represented the act of finding final peace after a life of trials and anxieties.

Riley, then, should not be taken as an outright villain, even though before he appears onstage, Rose's fear about the stranger in the basement has imbued him with the quality of terror. There is

[1] Martin Esslin, *The Theatre of the Absurd* (Garden City, New York, 1961), p. 201.

irony in the play, however, and the actor who portrays Riley should not fasten on his threatening features, but rather endeavor to bring out Riley's poignant quality. He speaks to Rose always tenderly, never insidiously; Rose's insults and Bert's attack seem undeserved. Riley is victim as well as usurper.

The relationships in *The Room* are more complicated than they appear at first glance. Bert, younger and unready for death, is selfishly unwilling to let Rose leave, though she seems on the verge of accepting Riley's invitation. Bert, therefore, is something of a usurper, keeping Rose cut off from her past, her family, even her true identity—Riley calls her Sal, and after much inner struggle Rose tacitly acknowledges the name. Bert would hold her a willing prisoner, morbidly afraid of the outside world; his closing the curtains upon his return to the room is significant in this respect; he himself sees something of the outside on his tours in his motor van, experiences he enjoys almost like secret liaisons. At the start of the play Bert treats Rose quite distantly, much as Stanley treats doting Meg in *The Birthday Party*. Once his secure situation is endangered, however, Bert reacts violently, but futilely. I do not mean to suggest that Bert, in seeking to prevent Rose from leaving, although it may be for her a beneficial departure, ought to be recast in the role of villain. Bert's action is understandable and pardonable. In Pinter's work a pattern declares itself in which characters whose security becomes undermined struggle hysterically to maintain it, no matter how flippantly and pridefully they have taken it for granted hitherto.

The Room can also be understood as a psychodrama in which the room itself represents the island of conscious security afloat upon a dark sea of forgotten memories and vague wishes. Pinter renders the apartment building as Kafka might: impossibly large, so that the landlord, if he is the landlord, no longer remembers how many floors it has. On this level of psychological symbolism, Riley's emergence from the basement may represent the rising of an unconscious impulse in Rose to return home to a haven of true security. To take Bert as a usurper is to assert that in his first play Pinter accomplished one of his most interesting variations on the theme of usurpation, for it is only at the end of the play that we see Bert's wish for security faulting Rose's freedom which has lain dormant for years. Not until the end can we see that the security of the room is an unsatisfactory condition, a retreat from life more fully lived. In later plays such as *A Slight Ache* and *The Homecoming* the necessity of leading an active, meaningful life rather than a withdrawn, self-protective one is clearly implied. The gradual exposition which comes in *The Room* is a technique which pervades Pinter's work. John Russell Brown points out that Pinter's plays are wholly expository, and only incidentally, if at all, development and conclusion.[2] Thus the final revelations of Rose, Bert, and Riley force us to reassess initial impressions.

The theme of usurpation is also broached in Pinter's first full-length play, *The Birthday Party,* written, like *The Room,* in 1957. The principal character, Stanley, has secured himself in a seaside boarding house where he is cared for by an elderly woman, Meg, in a half motherly, half sensual way. The usurpers in this case are two sinister figures, Goldberg and McCann, who arrive at the house in search of Stanley. Precisely why Stanley has been pursued is never clarified, although references to an organization he has "betrayed" and many remarks about Ireland suggest, as one critic notes, that Stanley has acted as traitor to the I.R.A.[3] Such speculations are not important, however, for it is not essential to pinpoint specific reasons for the pursuit; the play is not primarily interesting for its narrative line, or even any symbolic meaning which might be attached to the series of bizarre events; unlike *The Room* and *The Dumb Waiter, The Birthday Party* does not rely on "gimmicky" devices, more amateurish and facilely contrived. Like Beckett's *Waiting for Godot,* the play explores a situation whose significance is suggested rather than stated, and which, as Esslin says, presents a valid poetic image immediately seen as relevant and true. "It speaks plainly of the individual's pathetic search for security; of secret dreads and anxieties; of the terrorism of our world. . . ."[4]

The attack of Goldberg and McCann against Stanley takes the form of verbal assault, and the brainwashing to which Stanley is subjected is an excellent example of Pinter's use of language as an instrument of power. In a staccato series of insults and perplexing questions, Stanley's world is undermined and he is brought into a

[2] John Russell Brown, "Mr. Pinter's Shakespeare," reprinted in *Essays in the Modern Drama,* ed. Morris Freedman (Boston, 1964), p. 352.

[3] James T. Boulton, "Harold Pinter: *The Caretaker* and Other Plays," *Modern Drama,* VI (September, 1963), p. 136.

[4] Martin Esslin, *op. cit.,* p. 205.

state of nervous shock; he is accused of killing his wife, then reproached for never marrying, but jilting his bride at the church; this attack on his character is followed by a medley of theo-philosophical challenges, as Goldberg demands, "Do you recognise an external force, responsible for you, suffering for you?" then launches into a harangue on the necessity or possibility of the number 846, insisting that necessity must precede possibility; ultimately Stanley's very existence is assailed: "You're dead. You can't live, you can't think, you can't love. You're dead." The absurd inquisition breaks down Stanley's defenses and undermines his self. At the birthday party that evening—ironically Goldberg comments how wonderful a thing birth is, and ought to be celebrated—Stanley's disintegration is complete, and in the darkness of the scene his own dark impulses surface when he tries to strangle Meg and rape the neighbor, Lulu. In a stupor of insanity next morning, Stanley is led away by Goldberg and McCann.

Pinter evokes a mood of terror and mystery by creating a distorted world in which the reasons for events are suppressed, and the trivial daily affairs of life give rise to the most passionate actions and revelations. The relationship between the usurpers and usurped in *The Birthday Party* is simply aggressive. The work is more polished than *The Room,* and may be better for lacking that play's perhaps accidental ambiguity. The poignant effect of *The Birthday Party* is to stress the impossibility of an individual's finding security in a sanctuary beyond his past. It is more clearly established in this play than in *The Room* that the past from which Stanley has fled was a frightening one which deserves to be banished. In both plays our attention is focussed principally on those characters who are the objects of usurpation; even in *The Dumb Waiter,* also written in 1957, where the central figures are usurpers, hired killers, by trade, our concern is for them as characters against whom a usurpation is being carried out by the mysterious being at the other end of the dumb waiter. However, in the last act of *The Birthday Party* there is an indication that Pinter's focus is in process of shifting from the usurped to the usurpers as well. With Stanley's collapse, the climax of the play, occurring in Act II, Pinter devotes his final act to revealing the fears and insecurities of the aggressors, Goldberg and McCann. The implication is that even the usurpers are bereft, with secrets to hide and fears to repress. The secluded house of *The Birth-*

day Party corresponds to the situation in *The Room,* while Goldberg and McCann parallel the henchmen, Ben and Gus, in *The Dumb Waiter,* which might serve as a one-act sequel to the longer play. With *The Caretaker,* perhaps Pinter's finest play thus far, the central situation becomes the interplay of mutual needs and fears, love and hate between the aggressive and retreating figures. Pinter's usurpers evolve from merely aggressive figures to characters latently insecure who seek a form of security by parastically fastening on their victims.

A pattern of violence declares itself in Pinter's first plays—visible violence in *The Room* and *The Dumb Waiter,* imminent in *The Birthday Party*. Violence overtakes those characters who have fled active commitment in life and have failed to attain a stronger, more intimate truth in human relationships. Pinter has revealed that he originally planned to end *The Caretaker* with the violent death of Davies, but came to realize that violence was not necessary. Pinter regards *The Caretaker* as a progression in his art: "I have no need to use cabaret turns and blackouts and screams in the dark to the extent that I enjoyed using them before. I feel that I can deal, without resorting to that kind of thing, with a human situation." [5] The separation between Aston and Davies at the end of *The Caretaker* suggests the tragic loneliness suffered by persons unable to transcend personal egoism and enter self-sacrificingly upon the rewarding relationship needed by both. Blame for this failure, if blame can properly be assessed in a tragic world, lies chiefly with Davies, but the important fact is that failure to achieve a positive relationship injures both characters.

Aston helps Davies, a vagabond, by sharing his lodgings, not simply out of pity, but also out of a need for companionship. When Aston opens his soul to Davies and tells of his experience in a mental hospital where he received electric-shock treatment, Davies tries to use the information against him by playing off Aston against his brother, Mick. His attempt fails, and Aston forces him to leave, the play closing with Davies begging for another chance to stay in Aston's room. The request is to be understood as futile, a final separation about to take place. In this play the usurper, Davies, fails in the end, and this points up the ambivalence of Pinter's

[5] Harold Pinter, interview with Kenneth Tynan, B.B.C. Home Service (October 28, 1960). Cited in Martin Esslin, *op. cit.,* p. 212.

attitude: there is sympathy for aggressor and victim alike, for there is no true villain in a Pinter play.

The relationship between Aston and Mick differs from the situation of isolated security in *The Room* and *The Birthday Party.* The brothers are not intimately close, nor protective of each other, either mutually or singly; there is nothing of the quasi-parental relationship between Rose and Bert or Meg and Stanley. Aston probably could not reveal his past to Mick as he does to the stranger, Davies. Mick appears a more willful, belligerent character than Aston, mocking and taunting Davies throughout the play. Toward the end, however, it becomes clear that Mick too is not entirely secure. When Davies tells him that his brother is "nutty, half way gone," the remark triggers in Mick panicky reflections which suggest his inability to accept and cope with his brother's condition:

> *He hurls the Buddha against the gas stove. It breaks.* (*Passionately.*) Anyone would think this house was all I got to worry about. I got plenty of other things I can worry about. . . . I'm not worried about this house. I'm not interested. My brother can worry about it. . . . I thought I was doing him a favour, letting him live here. He's got his own ideas. Let him have them. I'm going to chuck it in.

Immediately following, Aston enters and the brothers face each other, "smiling, faintly." Mick begins to speak, cannot, and leaves. He has been forced to a painful recognition of his own and his brother's dilemmas, and for a moment they understand each other. But they must move apart, aware of the gulf between them and unable to shape a more intimate bond.[6]

The pace of *The Caretaker* is smoother than *The Birthday Party,* for Pinter's manner of continuous exposition more neatly adapts to the movement of events; there is no midway climax followed by a final act of posterior character study. *The Caretaker* stresses the helplessness of people to develop meaningful relationships because of innate pride and selfishness; an ironic pun exists in the play's title, for Davies, needy as he is, completely fails to "take care." Not satisfied with the job of caretaker, he seeks to dispossess Aston. Ambition is his tragic flaw. The security which he desperately needs is thwarted by his own pride and superiority. Davies is one of Pinter's

[6] I am partly indebted for my interpretation of this scene to John Russell Brown, *op. cit.*, p. 354.

most skillfully drawn characters. He might be considered a tragicomic figure in the tradition of Chaplin's tramp, were it not for his excessive vanity and lack of good-nature. The combination of aggressive egoism and abject servitude—qualities, incidentally, which are shared by Barrett in *The Servant,* who can one moment exert himself fully to gain the upper hand over his master, and the next moment sincerely plead to be forgiven an offense—is comic, true, and sad. Pinter's most successful characters are round, complex figures, who, while their motivations and backgrounds may be vague, are thoroughly alive and complete in the onstage present.

The usurpers discussed thus far have been active in their roles, whether these have been rolls of aggressive persecution (Goldberg and McCann) or of struggle to reach a state of personal security at someone else's expense (Davies). The best example of a "passive" usurper is the Matchseller in Pinter's one-act radio play, *A Slight Ache.* The Matchseller, whom Edward and Flora invite into their country home after watching him stand outside for weeks, remains totally silent, but elicits the private fears and wishes of the two. Edward is seen to be spiritually dry, while Flora's latent sexual vitality brims to the surface. Eventually the Matchseller replaces Edward as Flora's husband. Stylistically less realistic than *The Caretaker,* the play has a mystifying element resembling Pinter's first short works, especially in the bizarre conclusion where the Matchseller displaces Edward. The title refers to a gradually growing pain in Edward's eyes, which suggests his deteriorating vitality, if eyes may be taken as the symbol of spiritual and masculine vigor. In Pinter's work, poor eyesight and blindness appear to be signs of a sterile inner state which may be equivalent to death; the motif appears in *The Room* and *The Birthday Party,* where Goldberg smashes Stanley's glasses, without which Stanley is virtually blind, and death promises to follow. In *A Slight Ache,* Edward's remark that he slept "uninterrupted as usual" is also significant for Pinter's general symbolism: dreamlessness is another sign of the lack of vital inner life. In *The Caretaker,* Davies insists that he never dreams; a dream is a threat to security. Davies may be unconscious of any night thoughts, but that he does dream and that his nights are not so secure as he would have them is ironically apparent from the amount of tossing and groaning he does every night.

In *A Slight Ache,* Edward has withdrawn into a placid, backwater existence: his only interest is in writing theological and philosophical articles; he and Flora pass their time in asinine small talk about the convolvulus, japonica, and honeysuckle. In the meeting with the Matchseller, as Edward's security crumbles, his identity is challenged. He tells his wife, "You're deluded. And stop calling me Edward." That his withdrawal has been a fearful retreat from the challenges of interpersonal relations becomes clear when he reflects, "my life was accounted for, . . . my progress was fluent, after my long struggling against all kinds of usurpers, disreputables, lists, literally lists of people anxious to do me down, and my reputation down, my command was established, all summer I would breakfast. . . ."

Pinter would seem to be suggesting that direct involvement, intellectually and interpersonally, is necessary for life to be truly meaningful and truly secure. In *The Dumb Waiter* and *The Birthday Party* he has Ben and Goldberg comment on the need of developing "interests" in order for life to be pleasant; the interests enumerated by Ben are trivial, and while, coming from him, the moral seems comic, it is actually one which Pinter holds quite seriously. In Pinter's most recent drama, *The Homecoming,* the theme of intellectual isolation is even more prominent. Teddy, a professor of philosophy, and his wife Ruth make a surprise visit from the United States, where Teddy teaches, to his family home in England. The household, governed by Teddy's father, includes Ted's uncle and two brothers. The family eventually entice Ruth away from her husband by offering to set her up as part-time prostitute, with special duties toward her in-laws. But having usurped Teddy's wife, which he unemotionally accepts, the family suddenly realize that they themselves may have been usurped—by Ruth. Teddy's aged father mutters, "I've got a funny idea she'll do the dirty on us, you want to bet? She'll use us, she'll make use of us, I can tell you!"

The motif of the "safe room" still appears in *The Homecoming,* but Pinter has given stronger emphasis to intellectual rather than environmental isolation in concentrating on Teddy's predicament. As in *A Slight Ache,* the opening breach between Teddy and Ruth stems from incompatibility between her latent sexual vitality and his intellectual quietude. Even his career has grown humdrum—he is a detached specialist in his field. When his formally uneducated brother Lenny asks, "Do you detect a certain logical incoherence in the central affirmations of Christian theism?"—the sort of hyper-serious question Pinter enjoys putting into the mouths of unlikely speakers—Teddy replies, "That question doesn't fall within my province." Though Lenny presses his philosophical inquiry, Teddy brushes him off. It is Ruth who becomes engaged in the discussion, and while her remarks lack philosophical sophistication and serve more to reveal her dominant sexuality, they do demonstrate a practical and vital concern in such questions which her husband lacks. An apparent tendency in Pinter's work is the use of intellectual types, which would permit a more direct treatment or intimation of philosophical issues; heretofore, as in *The Birthday Party,* such themes could be made explicit only by slipping half-absurd comments such as Goldberg's on necessity and possibility into the stream of the dialogue.

The variation on the theme of usurpation which comes in *A Slight Ache* and *The Homecoming* involves the suggestion that a secure, "professorial" existence which resists life's challenges becomes a sterile condition, vulnerable to destruction. Despite the bizarre outcome of *The Homecoming,* it is among Pinter's most realistic plays, and represents in at least one respect a departure from his earlier technique: the past of these characters is far more fully sketched in, rather than being left vague and mysterious. The information we receive explains in large part their present interest in obtaining Ruth.

Pinter's handling of the theme of usurpation is still evolving. One of the primary sources of the theme is Robin Maugham's novella, *The Servant* (1949), which Pinter has adapted as a screenplay. (The usurping servant is a theme with even older antecedents—Dickens's diabolical lawyer, Tulkinghorn, in *Bleak House,* for instance, a character who preys on knowledge about his aristocratic employer as a means, not of gaining practical power over him, but rather as a means of possessing his soul, usurping his life.) *The Servant* tells the story of the spiritual and physical decline of a well-to-do young man whose love of comfort and weakness of purpose lead him to become dominated and manipulated by his manservant, Barrett. Pinter's version corresponds to the main lines of the plot of the original, and the only significant changes in characters involve the removal of a first-person narrator, who is often awkward in accounting for how facts of the story came to his attention, and the incorporation of an affair which develops between Barrett and his master's girlfriend—this usurpation by Barrett does not occur in the novella.

Pinter transforms a clumsy conventional story, where character and motivation are thoroughly defined and explicated, into a subtle, ambiguous drama where villain and victim cannot be catalogued so simply. Pinter's *Servant* is a more frightening and mysterious experience. The decision to remove the first-person narrator, despite his integral connection with the characters and events of the original story, gives the play an independent life beyond the objective, analytical, controlling presence of the narrator; we are allowed to make our own judgments of the entangled relationships. In Pinter's work, the situation between master and servant comes to be seen as one based on mutual needs; it is pathetic that the servant's disdainful pride and the master's moral weakness prevent them from attaining the proper, mutually helpful master-servant relationship; instead, both lapse into a decadent state, with Barrett gaining the upper hand. In Maugham's story Barrett is presented as unmitigatedly wicked; in Pinter's screenplay there is greater ambiguity, and sympathetic understanding is allowed both for the conquered master and the triumphant servant. It is worthwhile comparing Maugham's and Pinter's versions of the scene in the pub where Barrett begs his master to take him back after being dismissed. For Maugham, Barrett here is simply a conniving, hypocritical scoundrel; for Pinter, it is difficult to determine whether Barrett's pleading is not sincere, for, like Davies, outside his patron's house he is hopelessly adrift, and this desperate insecurity can spark pitiable fear and sincere contrition. The scene in the pub parallels the closing scene of *The Caretaker.*

Given a threatening, hostile world, the fearful insecurity of characters like Barrett and Davies causes them to seek security at the expense of others. In Pinter's more ambitious plays, where the usurper is not merely an external agent endangering a situation of seemingly secure withdrawal, the implication is that men are prevented from reaching rewarding relationships, wherein the truest security lies, by their own selfishness, pride, or weakness. In some plays Pinter also stresses the need of vital commitment in order to lead a meaningful life. The loneliness of man roots from his own faults and fears. The wall of isolation he seeks to build around himself as a means of security represents either a futile effort to escape, as in *The Birthday Party,* or a sterile, passive condition, as in *A Slight Ache.* At the end of *The Birthday Party,* after Stanley has been taken away, as Meg relives the previous night's celebration, without comprehending the terrible experience Stanley has undergone, and without even realizing that he is gone, we have one of Pinter's most poignant expressions of the failure of understanding and tragedy of loneliness which define the relations among men.

If usurpation represents the basic relationship between Pinter's characters, the use of language as an instrument of power is the usurper's principal means of aggression. The style of Pinter's dialogue is ordinarily spoken of in connection with "theatre of the absurd." Pinter captures the irrelevancy and vapidity of everyday speech, and this suggests a preoccupation with the theme of non-communication, a favorite topic of Beckett and Ionesco, the two writers in the mainstream of absurd theatre. In Pinter, failure to communicate significantly mirrors the even more significant failure to achieve satisfactory personal relationships. Pinter does not believe that communication is impossible, but fearful: "I feel that instead of any inability to communicate there is a deliberate evasion of communication. Communication itself between people is so frightening that rather than do that there is a continual cross-talk, a continual talking about other things, rather than what is at the root of their relationship." [7] Failure to communicate is a sign of man's isolation within himself. The difficulty of achieving positive personal relationships is a theme which has been treated by many modern writers, among them E. M. Forster, D. H. Lawrence, and James Joyce. Where the effort to establish these relationships ends in failure, we have a peculiarly modern sort of tragedy. A hostile world and man's very nature prevent the solace of love or friendship from being found.

Pinter has adopted certain conventions and techniques of the absurd dramatists, especially in early plays like *The Room* and *The Dumb Waiter.* But he stands outside the main current of this theatre, and, if his latest play, *The Homecoming,* is a valid indica-

[7] Harold Pinter, interview with Kenneth Tynan, *op. cit.*, p. 207.

tion, he is tending toward even more realistic drama. Nearly all of his work lacks the viciously grotesque quality of much absurd theatre, though as a serious artist he has naturally been influenced by the themes and methods of the avant-garde playwrights.

Martin Esslin points out that Pinter is in search of a higher degree of realism for the theatre, rejecting the theory of the "well-made play" because it provides too much information about the backgrounds and motivations of the characters.[8] In Pinter, as in life, it is extremely difficult to know the vital, secret facts of a character's past that determine present actions. Pinter's characters often give contradictory information about themselves, making it hard to know anything for certain about them. Pinter has said, "The desire for verification is understandable but cannot always be satisfied. There are no hard distinctions between what is real and what is unreal, nor between what is true and what is false. The thing is not necessarily true or false. It can be both true and false." Because of this ambiguity, it is often difficult to evaluate characters and their actions; furthermore, it is dangerous to insist on a single interpretation of a given play. Pinter's work, like Beckett's, can be significant on many levels.

[8] Martin Esslin, *op. cit.*, p. 206.

Harold Pinter's Happy Families

by R. F. Storch

The shock-tactics of Harold Pinter's dramaturgy are so effective that his audience, cowed into the pit of irrationality, is afraid to ask why in the name of anxiety it has succumbed, and what it is in the plays that gives them such insidious power. To ask the question at all may seem silly, because Pinter, we know, deliberately destroys all clues for a rational appraisal: the irrationality is the major part of the meaning. Everyone has of course experienced the menace and terror and loneliness which are generally applauded as Pinter's chief dramatic effects. It is not only drama critics who by sheer repetition have made us accept anxiety and alienation as the final account of experience. And yet we are right to ask the question, because the very deliberateness with which Pinter befuddles us hints at an ordered meaning which will satisfy the rational levels of our minds. Anxiety is a word to conjure with these days, but what it pulls out of the hat is only the shadow of a meaning. And if we are honest with ourselves, we have to admit that the state of shock is enjoyable only if sooner or later rational relief is in sight.

In spite of the clever dislocation of common sense, Pinter's plays affect us because they are about the middle-class family, both as sheltering home longed for and dreamed of, and as many-tentacled monster strangling its victim. It does not, after all, surprise us that there is more menace and irrationality in this dramatic material than in any other. The London stage since 1945 (to look no further) has been very much occupied with the family as a trap-door to the underworld. Whether the angle of descent has been religious, as in Graham Greene, or social class, as in Osborne and Wesker, the game of Happy Families has provided the entertainment. Pinter,

"Harold Pinter's Happy Families" by R. F. Storch. From *The Massachusetts Review,* 8 (Autumn 1967), 703–12.

however, is by far the most radical in breaking with the naturalistic conventions of *drame bourgeois*. For he burrows into dark places where it is of little consequence whether a family is working-class or professional. If he is obsessed by the peculiar horrors of middle-class families, this is not within the larger view of social class, but simply because they epitomize everything that is horrifying in any family situation today. He makes us see that class distinctions are curiously out of date for today's theatre, and that a kitchen sink is no more enlightening than a coffee table. When such paraphernalia are made into class-symbols, they merely hide what Pinter knows to be the real drama. We cling to kitchen sinks in the belief that at last we have reached something solid and honest; but Pinter will have none of that. He destroys the predictable place of things, deliberately confuses and contradicts. As soon as a situation looks as if it were attaining a recognizable meaning, he introduces some nonsense, wild improbability or verbal play, and we fall once more through the trap-door. His plays consist largely of his dogged attempts to destroy consistency and any clue to a rational pattern. The act of writing becomes, then, the work of the repressive censor as much as what is usually thought of as the creative imagination. This would seem to account for the taste of ashes, the sterility which pervades not only Pinter's plays but the whole Theatre of the Absurd in spite of its wildly fantastic ingredients. But the interesting point about this censorship is that it in fact underlines, or at any rate circumscribes, the very clues it destroys. As a result the audience is insidiously attacked at a level where it hurts most.

Pinter's plays are largely about the running away from certain family situations, and the faster the running, the clearer it becomes what he is running away from. Every trick in his repertory is supposed to distract our attention from those unappeasable furies haunting his mind. But their faces, or masks, leer and glower from the plays all the same. By dislocating our attention from the common sense view of things he makes us alive to primitive fears, destroys the rational façade of the adult mind, and lays bare regressive fantasies. He does not put to secondhand use ancient myths, in the manner of Cocteau or Sartre, but discovers the infantile fears that lie at the roots of those myths, and that are the ultimate nourishment of the poetic imagination.

There is another level to his plays, one he himself has drawn attention to. Much of what strikes us as irrational, comic or even idiotic, he says, he has merely set down as actually observed. The way people talk at or past each other, have breakfast together, or discuss the furnishing of a room is quite extraordinary enough if it is set down without embellishment or literary convention. But this strangeness of the ordinary Pinter uses as a way into the more fearful strangeness of the usually hidden.

The breakfast scene at the beginning of *The Birthday Party* (1959) is a brilliant example of inane small talk leading into fantasies and infantile terrors. This early play is one of the most concentrated, as it were single-minded, of Pinter's achievements. Stanley, in his role of boarder, is very clearly and lucidly at the psychological centre of the action. He has run away from home, only to hole himself up in another home-like shelter. And Meg, his landlady, sustains, more directly than a mother probably could, the ambivalent feeling of a mother towards her son. Stanley daydreams of his one and only concert, which has been a great success: "My father nearly came down to hear me. Well, I dropped him a card anyway. But I don't think he could make it. No, I — I lost the address, that was it." The dialogue moves through the neurotic realm of what could have been true into sheer invention. What emerges is that Stanley was not going to give his first concert in his father's presence. But the neurotic mind is honest in its own fashion: keeping away father must be followed by retribution: they carved Stanley up. He went down to his next place, but "the hall was closed, the place was shuttered up, not even a caretaker. They'd locked it up. . . . They want me to crawl down on my bended knees." Stanley's career as concert-pianist is effectively "blocked" and he, the guilty son, dare not leave his bolthole. "There is nowhere to go," he says to Lulu, the local bit of goods, but it really means that he is afraid to go, even to imagine somewhere to go. Father might turn up. As it happens, he does, in the shape of Goldberg, who makes up to the girl. When Goldberg and McCann enter, there is at first some rather cheap mystification; they use the language of gangsters: "Is this it?" — "This is it." But the real threat they are to Stanley soon becomes clear. Goldberg reminisces of his childhood in a cosy, prosperous Jewish middle-class family. Uncle Barney has a house "just outside Basingstoke at the time. Respected by the whole community." The menace comes from this all-enveloping cosiness, the family culture served up in a heavy syrup of sentimentality. McCann's version is of the familiar Irish kind. (James Joyce's young man had to escape from it too, though it continued to haunt him.) Goldberg and McCann make a "team"—enterprising, loyal, and doing a job. Not necessarily a criminal job. The point is that any job done in this team spirit becomes sinister. They see each other as, respectively, "a capable man" and "a man in your position." And we know what skullduggery that sort of backscratching often hides. The team spirit belongs to the same world as family sentiment: both reach out their tentacles to strangle Stanley. The two visitors menace him with conformity, and the play shows how they crush him. The psychological lever is to make Stanley regress to the infantile state, where the need for security, mother, home and respectability—being "one of us"—becomes so overpowering that he is brainwashed of the last vestiges of an independent spirit. Goldberg is one long, sickening repertory of bourgeois make-believe, while McCann is the bird-brained muscleman (all sentiment, too) who wields the truncheon, like a good storm trooper, when Stanley is not regressing fast enough into the infantile fold. The birthday party celebrates Stanley's infancy, something like his fifth year. The toy drum is unpacked, Stanley plays it, and the music possesses him. He beats the drum savagely. Motherly Meg asks for a kiss. She wants to keep him for her boy. Before he kisses her, his shoulders sag. But he is not yet defeated; he leaps at her throat.

Act II begins with the third temptation (the first is motherly Meg, the second treacly Goldberg): namely, McCann's boyish truculence, daring you to step across the line he has drawn, or shouldering you in a crowd. He is the son Stanley should have been: go-ahead, tough, part of the team. The interrogation dramatizes the pressure from Stanley's background and upbringing; the world of respectability becomes a terrorizing cross-examination. It is not real moral problems that constitute the menace but petty trespasses and finally a childish puzzle: why did the chicken cross the road; and which came first, the chicken or the egg. This produces the kind of worry a child might have in facing the adult world. Goldberg's speech in Act III parodies prudential morality: the rule of thumb, the decent way of life; but it is all meaningless. He is unable to finish his line beginning, "Because I believe that the world. . . ." A later parody of the code—work hard and play hard—is more than half way to idiocy. It prepares us for Stanley's final entrance, brainwashed and totally idiotic. He is now the suitable subject for the trite baits of the ad age: anything from an abdominal belt to a yacht. When he is about to be taken away, Petey pleads with him: "Stan, don't let them tell you what to do!" But it is too late, for Stanley, by way of infantile regression into the bosom of the family, has become the perfect victim for anyone who wants to tell him what to do.

The most devastating moment in the play is the last. Meg is completely oblivious of what had happened at the party, and quite unaware of the terrible things she has done to her Stanley. All she remembers is that she was the belle of the evening. At the end of the play hate of the female burns with a hot acetylene flame.

The Caretaker (first staged in 1960) does not have a woman in it, and apparently no one to take the place of father. And yet mother and father are like ghosts haunting the room, which is really the main character of the play. Its subject might be called: who is to occupy the room, and what sort of person is a caretaker—the substitute for parental care. Davies is as stupid as Meg, as garrulous and helpless. He is menaced, speaks of being maltreated and attacked. Put him into a pinafore and he is a housewife. He is always disgusted; it is the tenor of his dialogue. He nags like a woman: "My job's cleaning the floor, clearing the tables, doing a bit of washing-up, nothing to do with taking out buckets!" He is curiously epicene. Like Meg he is impervious to everything but his own needs, completely selfish and self-absorbed. The most powerful emotion emerging in the play is hatred of his kind of stupidity. His whining ungratefulness is particularly repulsive. "Can't wear shoes that don't fit. Nothing worse. I said to this monk, here, I said, look here, mister. . . ." His trying on a pair of boots becomes a nauseous spectacle.

Aston is also a weak character, fiddling about the room, making the bed. (Pinter's plays often have two contrasted male characters, one strong, one weak. Mick and Aston in this play; Ben and Gus in *The Dumb Waiter;* Goldberg and McCann in *The Birthday Party;* Max and Sam in *The Homecoming.*) Aston, unlike Mick, is not sure whether he has a right to occupancy. He had been betrayed by his mother into a serious brain operation that left him permanently disabled. The operation was performed with something like "pincers." As Act II ends with castration, so Act I had ended with a rape. Mick, the strong, threatening character, screws back Davies' arm and forces him to the floor, *"struggling, grimacing, whimpering and staring."* Mick remains silent. His gesture of placing a finger on his lips and then on Davies' dramatizes this silence and at the same time underlines the sexual meaning of the struggle. Next Mick examines the bed and Davies' trousers. He presses him down with his foot. The first words he utters are equivocal: "What's the game?"

The opening of Act II is a good example of deliberate nonsense putting a blind between a vague feeling of menace and its cause in an obviously sexual tension. Mick cross-examines Davies—did you sleep in that bed, how did you sleep. This examination is repeated several times but interspersed with long monologues of utter nonsense. The bed becomes more significant: at first it was his, later it is his mother's. "Now don't get perky, son, don't get perky. Keep your hands off old mum."

One cannot push character-analysis very far in Pinter's plays. *The Caretaker,* for example, does not sort out motivation or lines of action by giving them consistently to one or the other character. Instead of an interplay of fixed characters we have a kaleidoscope of pieces of experience: of memories, fears and hatreds, which every now and then get shaken into configurations of character and situation. Even the division between the sexes is unstable. Davies' job comes close to a housewife's and he often talks like one: "You want me to do all the dirty work all up and down them stairs, just so I can sleep in this lousy filthy hole every night?" Mick at first seems to listen sympathetically, but consequently seems to enjoy all the more telling Davies with sheer and open cruelty that he is not wanted. The quarrel becomes violent (Mick smashes the Buddha) and sounds more and more like a marital fight. Davies: "All right then . . . you do that . . . you do it . . . if that's what you want. . . ." Mick: "Anyone would think this house was all I got to worry about. . . ." At the end the brothers unite and throw Davies out. At least half of him sounds like a deserted and maltreated woman.

Whatever situations and characters Pinter invents, the obsessive patterns will turn up. In *A Slight Ache* Edward has achieved respectability (like Goldberg) and wants to turn back to the point in his youth where he could have taken a different turning (like

Stanley). His advice to the enigmatic dummy of a matchseller, who becomes whatever is most desired or feared or regretted, is very much like Goldberg's formula: keep your shoulder to the wheel, etc. Flora tells of her being raped, the one experience that seems to be meaningful to her, and makes up to the matchseller as Meg does to Stanley: "It's me you were waiting for, wasn't it? You've been waiting for me. You've seen me in the woods, picking daisies, in my apron, my pretty daisy apron, and you came and stood, poor creature, at my gate, till death do us part. Poor Barnabas. I'm going to put you to bed. I'm going to put you to bed and watch over you. But first you must have a whacking great bath. And I'll buy you pretty little things that will suit you. And little toys to play with. On your deathbed. Why shouldn't you die happily?" The role of woman, as Pinter sees her, put in a nutshell.

A Night Out is a dull play (BBC, 1960) because the theme is out in the open. Albert's mother is as nagging as Davies, as possessive as Meg and as deadly as Flora. The play becomes witty in Act III, when the prostitute turns out to be a respectable mother: at that Alfred explodes: "You are all the same, you see, you're all the same, you're just a dead weight round my neck. . . ." *The Dwarfs,* broadcast in the same year, is much more impressive because it belongs to the realm of disguised or displaced motivations. In many respects it resembles *The Caretaker,* except that it comes even closer to naked childhood obsessions, who are given the guise of dwarfs. The scene is again a domestic interior: there is talk of cleaning the place: "You'd think a man like that would have a maid, wouldn't you, to look after the place when he's away, to look after his milk?" And, "Still, he won't find much to come home to, will he? There's nothing in the kitchen, there's not even a bit of lettuce." And so on. The womanish complaints are given an irrational twist, but are still there—"I have to run downstairs to put the kettle on, run upstairs to finish what I am doing, run downstairs. . . ." This is the same Len who then meticulously and simplemindedly makes the room his own: "There is my table. That is a table. There is my chair. There is my table. . . ." The room is both an order and an ambush, a trap. A kingdom and an enemy. The imaginative pitch is so high that womanish chatter is reduced to a mechanical repetition: "What do I think of the cut? The cut? The cut? What a cut!" etc. The basic question is, "What are you doing in my room? What do you want here?" The answer comes from the king in his counting house: "I thought you might give me some bread and honey." But Len is afraid: "I don't want you to become too curious in this room. . . ." Indeed not, for rooms shrink, expand, and move. We have reached, very suddenly, the infantile fears and obsessions that will be embodied in the dwarfs. "But when the time comes, you see, what I shall do is place red hot burning coal in my own mouth." This cryptic statement is followed by *Silence* and "I've got some beigels." The situation becomes more clearly an anal fantasy. Len is told that he is not "elastic." "By elastic I mean being prepared for your own deviations." Pete's analysis of Len is highly suggestive of a very young child and is summed up very neatly in "You've got no idea how to preserve a distance between what you smell and what you think about. . . . How can you hope to assess and verify anything if you walk about with your nose stuck between your feet all day long?" The stage directions are clear enough: *Len begins to grunt spasmodically, to whimper, hiss, and by the end of the speech, to groan.* Pete's dream of peeling and blotched faces occasions Len's infantile whimpering. In the end it prompts the query of guilt: "Then I thought, Christ, what's my face like? Is that why she's staring? Is that rotting too?" Len, reduced to the infantile state, now sees the dwarfs in the cloaca: "They clock in very early, scenting the event. They are like kites in a city disguise." The cloaca then becomes the stock exchange: "All the same, it is essential that I keep a close watch on the rate of exchange, on the rise and fall of the market. . . . With due warning from them I shall clear my stocks, should there be a landslide." Here the obsession with fecal cleanliness comes very close to the surface. The obsession spreads. When the toasting fork drops on the hearth, Len shouts: "Don't touch it! You don't know what will happen if you touch it! You mustn't touch it! You mustn't bend!" His speech deteriorates into a child's perception of himself in a world he is not part of. The dwarfs are projections of his longing for "dirt": "One with a face of chalk chucks the dregs of the daytime into a bin and seats himself on the lid. He is beginning to chew though he has not eaten. Now they collect at the back step. They scrub their veins at the running sink, now they are gorged in the sud. . . ." And then the variations on "He sits. The other talks. He talks. The other sits. The other stands. I crouch." Len's fantasy continues until Mark asks: "What is up your nose now?" and Len answers: "I'm the centre of a holy plague." The plague is sent in punishment, and Len's occupancy of the room is threatened: "You are trying to buy and sell me . . . you're buying me out of house and home, you're a calculating bastard . . . I've lost a kingdom." (Again the nursery rhyme of the king in his counting house eating bread and honey.) The anal fantasy becomes more pronounced: "Always squatting and bending, dipping their wicks in the custard . . . then soothe each other's orifices with a local ointment. . . ." Lust and guilty fear become one: "It all came out, in about twenty-eight goes. I couldn't stop shivering and I couldn't stop squatting. . . ." Now the obsession with housecleaning at the beginning of the play is given meaning. At the very end, filth and disorder and the menace of change become identified: "And this change. All about me the change. The yard as I know it is littered with scraps of cat's meat . . . worms stuck in the poisoned shit heaps, the alleys a whirlpool of piss, slime, blood and fruit juice.—Now all is bare. All is clean. All is scrubbed. There is a lawn. There is a shrub. There is a flower."

To call *The Dwarfs* a *drame bourgeois* may seem stretching the term, but it is after all strictly accurate. For it deals with those infantile obsessions and fears which are the foundation of bourgeois virtues—cleanliness, order, four walls you can call your own. Many of the tensions in an Ibsen family are due to the frightful cost of taming the dwarfs, or to the reckless refusal to tame them.

Pinter's latest play *The Homecoming* (first performance, 1965) is an intriguing mixture of plain family drama at the naturalistic level and of obsessive fantasy which takes it out of the realm of the probable. At the naturalistic level Pinter has come into the open at last: the play deals with the tensions within a Jewish family. The central figure, the mother, is dead, and the father, Max, is the caretaker. The dead mother is still, however, the focus of all the emotions, even though she is not mentioned very often. Her ghost hovers in the background, and respect is paid to her memory. But that is only lip service. For the real emotions she has roused in her family are fear and hatred. The outrageously improbable plot—to set up Ruth both as communal concubine for the whole family and to make her a prostitute to bring in money—is simply the family's revenge against mother. Already in Act I, Lenny, with his stories of violence he has inflicted on women who threatened his health or had been inconsiderate, works off his hatred of Ruth as a mother figure. When they are introduced to each other, he won't accept the fact that she is married to Teddy, his brother. Max, the father, behaves equally irrationally, by calling her a prostitute. Ruth is consequently initiated into the family. Joey goes upstairs with her for two hours (though he does not "go the whole hog" with her) while Lenny tells stories of exploits in the Paddington area. But in the end Max's scheme of turning the tables on the woman at last, of getting the most out of her, instead of letting her use the family, seems no longer so easy. His assurance dwindles. "She'll use us, she'll make use of us, I can tell you!" He collapses and crawls to her knees where she is sitting surrounded by her subdued boys. The woman has won again.

The real power of Pinter's plays does not lie in the shock-tactics of the dramaturgy but in the terribly familiar situations they are supposed to draw our attention away from. We may not be aware of the obsessive fears of childhood which dominate Pinter's characters (or shadowy configurations that take the place of characters), but we are never far from them, and a Pinter play can trip us over into that neurotic world. The very shadowiness of the characterization makes his world more real, and makes it easier for us to enter it, to "identify." Pinter gets through to the level of neurotic obsessions by a radical break with conventional images of reality. He parodies the bourgeois life which plays out the neurosis. But his most remarkable achievement is that at his best his vision is not a fanciful distortion of reality, but has the effect of a more direct, honest understanding of it. This honesty is the strength of all original art; with Pinter it often reaches the extreme point of seeming naiveté: the pouring of a cup of tea, the reading of a newspaper can become events fraught with climactic meaning. These are not, however, symbolic actions; their significance is genuinely in their being lived. Pinter has a very strong sense of what people really experience (as against what literary convention says they experience), as well as a sense of the mystery contained in the trite and banal. In *The Room* (1960) the blind Negro is not a symbol, but the real instance of extreme loneliness, of human weakness, who calls to the woman, and who must be kicked to death by the man unable to face such weakness in a human being. The idea of the room itself occurs in most of Pinter's plays. It does not have to symbolize some abstraction of anxiety. The actual four walls are part of our most important experience: to be inside a room, or to be outside in the open spaces—this elementary contrast is probably as closely worked into our emotions as anything we can think of. By way of such outrageously simple imaginings Pinter arrives at the most direct and also the most harassing view of things, and the banal is forced to reveal its mystery. Every poet knows that the world of mysterious dreams is to be found at the very centre of banality. But the obverse is also true: the most terrifying anxieties are caused by commonplace occasions. Pinter's plays are not about menaces and anxieties in some metaphysical realm, but take their life from the very heart of reality, the bourgeois family. And whether we like it or not, nothing could be more real than that.

Pinter's *Homecoming:* The Shock of Nonrecognition

by Bert O. States

Teddy. You wouldn't understand my works. You wouldn't have the faintest idea of what they were about. You wouldn't appreciate the points of reference. You're way behind. All of you. There's no point in my sending you my works. You'd be lost. It's nothing to do with the question of intelligence. It's a way of being able to look at the world. It's a question of how far you can operate on things and not in things. I mean it's a question of your capacity to ally the two, to relate the two, to balance the two. To see, to be able to *see!* I'm the one who can see. That's why I can write my critical works. Might do you good . . . have a look at them . . . see how certain people can view . . . things . . . how certain people can maintain . . . intellectual equilibrium. Intellectual equilibrium. You're just objects. You just . . . move about. I can observe it. I can see what you do. It's the same as I do. But you're lost in it. You won't get me being . . . I won't be lost in it.

Blackout

I want to consider this play on what seems to me its most interesting level: that is, as a fiction about a group of people so *different* from us, while in certain obvious respects resembling us, that they are fascinating to watch. As a start, I propose to explore my recognition of the play in this speech which strikes me as being *there* in a peculiar way. It is, first, what we may call a genuine idea in a play that contains almost no ideas at all. Moreover, it is the only place in the play where Pinter permits a character to be un-

"Pinter's *Homecoming:* The Shock of Nonrecognition" by Bert O. States. From *The Hudson Review,* 21, no. 3 (August 1968), 474–86.

devious, "forthcoming" as Lenny would say, and that is a privilege most Pinter characters never get. Finally, as the penultimate break in the play, it is spoken with an almost thematic inflection. In fact, in the early throes of Critic's Rapture, I wondered whether Pinter wasn't very deliberately telling us more about *his Homecoming* here than about Teddy's.

Basically, the speech is Pinter's only pass at motivating Teddy's unusual capacity to "observe" with "equilibrium" the degeneration (or more correctly, the re-degeneration) of his wife to the level of his family. Applying it with a little imagination to *the rest* of Teddy, moreover, we can arrive at a coherent explanation for all of his actions: why he married a girl like Ruth, why he risked stopping off here en route back to the Campus from Venice, why he is willing (anxious, if you like) to return to the children without their mother, thus living out the pattern of his father's luck with Jessie. You can even predict, come twenty years, what intellectual barbarians the children will be, the eldest perhaps coming to a bad end in some dark form of father rejection. A New York psychoanalyst has suggested that Teddy is an example of a "totally withdrawn libido" troubled by a basic hatred for women and a tendency toward homosexuality (a family problem); he therefore substitutes intellectual equilibrium for a proper sex life. Michael Craig, who played Teddy, says he is the most violent of all the brothers, a veritable "Eichmann" underneath who has "rationalized his aggressions." Pinter, with characteristic simplicity (if not pure disinterest), says he walks out in the end to avoid a "messy fight," and anyway his marriage was on the rocks. All of these ideas (see *Saturday Review,* April 8, 1967) do not arise from the speech alone, of course, but the speech authorizes them: it puts the lid, so to speak, on Teddy's possibilities.

My feeling is that it is more a case of the play's not contradicting such ideas than of its actually containing them. Here is the one example of character "psychology" we get in the whole play and it directs us toward nothing definite in the character's experience but rather toward his *way of dealing* with whatever *happens* to be in his experience. In this respect, the speech bears out an impression confirmed by the rest of the play: the Pinter character's complete lack of interest in "things," in obligations, social or moral transactions, past "sins," future "goals," the whole world of palpable reality which Pinter is paradoxically so good at evoking in his dialogue; and his obsession with "points of reference," means, style, what can be *made* out of what is passing at any particular moment. In short, Teddy's philosophy of equilibrium is simply a more academic page out of the old family album.

In a more general sense, this helps to account for the powerful impression of the play's having been spun outward from an invisible center of complicity which clearly beckons the Interpreter to try his hand at supplying objective correlatives. On one hand, therefore, we explain the play as a study in psychic ambiguity: under the banal surface a massive Oedipal syndrome (like the part of the iceberg you can't see) bumps its way to grisly fulfillment. Or, beneath Freud lurks Jung and the archetypal: the father-sons "contest," the "fertility rite" on the sofa, the Earth Mother "sacrifice," the tribal sharing of her body (a Sparagmos for sure), the cyclical "return," and so on. But before the play is any or all of these things, it seems to be something much different and much simpler.

Perhaps the best way to pin it down is to try to say why psychology and myth seem unsatisfactory as explanations. The trouble with them is that they bring to the fore a purposiveness which seems at odds with the nature of the imagination we are dealing with. They assume that the play is *about* these things, whereas I think they come much closer to being by-products, as we would be dealing with by-products of, say, a story by Poe in the themes of crime-does-not-pay, or man-is-evil, or even in the mythic structure which I am sure there are plenty of in Poe, as there always are in tales of victimization. As for the psychological drives themselves, one somehow doubts that Pinter's characters, deep down, are any more troubled by appetites of the sexual kind than Dostoevsky's people are troubled by finding suitable jobs. They seem far more interested in manipulating the idea of sexuality, for its effect on others, than in their own performance. As for the mythic elements, it is simply hard to see what they prove, other than that Pinter deals in some pretty raw urges, hardly a distinction these days. To be "primitive" is not to be Pinteresque.

I suggest that it is in the peculiar way the story is told and in the liberties it takes with the reality it posits. For instance, if we reduce the play to its main turns of plot we have something like this: a son and his wife return to the family home on a visit abroad. Almost immediately, the father and brothers make open advances on the wife. She seems to tolerate, if not encourage, them and the husband makes no effort to protect his interests. In fact, it is the husband in the end who makes the family's proposal to the wife that she stay on as mother, mistress to everybody, and as prostitute. She accepts (!) and he goes back to their three children. We anticipate that it will be the wife who now controls the family.

It would be hard to conceive an action, in modern "family" terms, which violates so many of our moral scruples with so little effort and so little interest in making itself credible. You may read causes *into* it, but the causes pale beside the facts, like the page of repentance at the end of a dirty book. The whole thing has about it a blatant improbability and artifice which depends not upon our sympathizing, or understanding its origins, but upon our seeing how far it has taken its own possibilities. Moreover, it is all so harmless. As Eliot said of Ford's incest, the fact that such outrageous vices are defended by no one lends a color of inoffensiveness to their use. At any rate, the reaction one has to the play comes nowhere near Pity and Fear, or any of their weaker derivatives, but is better described as *astonishment at the elaboration.* And it is precisely this quality of astonishment that is apt to disappear from any thematically oriented recovery of the play.

So the idea I want to develop here is that *The Homecoming* may be about homecomings of all kinds but it is not ultimately about ours. We witness it, it even coaxes us to grope for connections among our own realities (and find them), but it does not, as its primary artistic mission, refer us back to a cluster of moral or existential issues we care very much about. What astonishes about the play is its taking of an extraordinarily brutal action, passing it through what is perhaps the most unobtrusive and "objective" medium since Chekhov's, and using it as the host for a peculiar activity of mind. We have invented special words for this activity ("Pintercourse," "Pinterism," "Pinterotic," etc.), which Pinter understandably detests, but it seems we have needed them as semantic consolation for his having hidden from us the thing they refer to.

And it is, I think, a thing—something all the characters *do* (in this play at least), with varying degrees of genius. To come back to my epigraph, what attracted me to Teddy's "philosophy" is that it offers the best explanation of this thing Pinter has given us. It is not particularly recondite, or mysterious; in fact, it goes under the household label of Irony, or the making of ironies, the art of being superior to things by disposing of them without passion or involvement. The best way to make the connection is to set Teddy's speech against this more clinical description of the ironic temper by Haakon Chevalier:

> The Ironist is committed to the search of a more and more exterior point of view, so as to embrace all contradictions and behold the world from a point of vantage to which nothing else is superior. The indefinite extension of his field of vision to the furthest attainable reaches is implied even in the point of view of the Ironic observer of a simple human situation. The Ironic reaction is exterior to both elements of the contrast observed. And this necessarily leads to a progressive extension of the point of view. Beyond the Ironist's perception of a situation is his Ironic perception of himself Ironically perceiving the situation, etc.

Now this fits and it doesn't fit, and I am ultimately more interested in the sense in which it fits Pinter's own perspective (and he, in turn, the contemporary perspective) than in its application to specific characters. It is a gentle kind of irony M. Chevalier deals with in his book about Anatole France, whereas ours is a more subterranean variety based in cruder contrasts. But it is the same operation, in essence, and as Chevalier goes on to observe, it accompanies a peculiar relationship to "everyday reality" and is "stimulated and encouraged to expression in a special environment." If you wish to think of it as the collective "motive" of the characters, and get your psychology in that way, it would certainly do no harm; but I think it has more aesthetic ramifications. For it seems to me that character is here usurping—rather wholesale—a privilege that has traditionally belonged to the audience (superiority to the situation) and that when irony is practiced to this degree of exclusiveness it might more properly be considered as a form of *audience* psychology designed by the author to meet the expectations of the "special environment" in which he writes, more about which later. This, in my opinion, is the source of our consternation and fascination with Pinter—our quest for the lost superiority of knowing more than the characters who now know more than we do, the very reverse of the familiar "dramatic" irony in which *we* know but they don't. To put it crudely, it is the goal of the Pinter character, as agent of his author's grand strategy, to stay ahead of the audience by "inventing" his drama out of the sometimes slender life afforded him (glasses of water, newspapers, cheese-rolls, etc.). His motto, in fact, might well be Renan's remark (which I also crib from Chevalier): "The universe is a spectacle that God offers himself; let us serve the intentions of the great choreogus by contributing to render the spectacle as brilliant, as varied as possible." To this end, he becomes, as it were, a little Pinter, an author of irony, sent into his incredible breathing world scarce half made-up, morally, to work on the proper business of his author's trade—to "trump" life, to go it one better by going it one worse. This, I think, is what Teddy is doing in his repressed, tweedy way in escorting his wife to the rank sweat of the family bed (which she, in turn, negotiates into a still greater triumph of "perspective") with all the possession of someone passing the salt. It is a similar triumph of perspective that moves Max to take one look at his eldest son and his wife, newly arrived from Independence America, the World's Bandwagon, and call her tart, smelly scrubber, stinking pox-ridden slut, a disease, sensing with uncanny instinct that his son is, at this moment, *bigger* than the family, outside it yet condescending to "visit," that his superiority is somehow vested in this woman and that an insult in the form of an imitation (not too convincing) of moral indignation will do the trick. It is, again, another triumph that his apology for this outrage should descend to an equally ludicrous imitation of fatherly sentimentality ("You want to kiss your old father? Want a cuddle with your old father?"). And so on, through his repertoire of sudden reversals of sentiment calculated to demonstrate that his perception of a situation includes all possible positions. For instance:

> He was fond of your mother, Mac was. Very fond. He always had a good word for her.
>
> *Pause.*
>
> Mind you, she wasn't such a bad woman. Even though it made me sick just to look at her rotten stinking face, she wasn't such a bad bitch. I gave her the best bleeding years of my life, anyway.

Finally, it is the pleasure of irony that moves the play's least gifted character, Sam, to spit out the priceless secret he has been nursing for years ("MacGregor had Jessie in the back of my cab as I drove them along") at a moment so right, so symmetrical, that the beauty of it almost kills him.

Pinter's best and most continuous irony, however, arises not from situation but from language, and on this point he reminds me a good deal of Chekhov and Beckett with whom he shares powerful affinities in imagination. Putting aside their differences, I think they are ironists in the same tradition, they hold similar fascination for us, and give us, on the whole, similar critical problems. They are probably the three least discursive playwrights one could name; in fact, their silence before the questions they raise—their Socratic smile, you might say—is so extreme that it qualifies as their special *excess,* like Genet's devout immorality, Brecht's social consciousness, Pirandello's cerebration. Such detachment is very rare in the theatre because it tends to produce the sort of play Hamlet might write, one that hovers on the verge of motionlessness (a quality for which all three have been variously praised or damned). Obviously their success with such essentially undramatic materials has a good deal to do with their preoccupation with words, silence (as anti-words), and with what we might broadly call the *expressive* aspect of life. And in each case it seems to me that even language functions in an ironic way, that our interest is centered upon a tension between the words and the situation. I was interested in Richard Gilman's article on *The Homecoming* in *The New York Times* (Jan. 22, 1967) in which he said that "language can itself be dramatic, can *be* the play, not merely the means . . . etc.," a remark which Mr. Simon trounced in *The Hudson Review* (Vol. 20, no. 1, Spring 1967) as intellectual cant. Now I don't think language can *be* the play any more than the medium can *be* the message, but there is something in Mr. Gilman's idea. I think he touches upon a habit of composition which Pinter has cultivated more and more as he goes along—a habit which is, in a technical sense, analogous to Chekhov's highly controlled practice of putting language out of proportion to the "content" (the almost *elegant* expression of near-suicidal desperation), and which we find again in Beckett's insistence on putting the significant things in the guise of insignificance ("What about hanging ourselves?"). The equivalent technique in Pinter—and especially in *The Homecoming* where it reaches a kind of *tour de force* intensity—is a direct and almost satirical formalism of expression which is, putting it mildly, inappropriate to the situation. The whole technique might be presampled in a remark Pinter himself recently made to a *Paris Review* reporter about politicians:

> I'll tell you what I really think about politicians. The other night I watched some politicians on television talking about Vietnam. I wanted very much to burst through the screen with a flamethrower and burn their eyes out and their balls off and then inquire from them how they would assess this action from a political point of view.

I checked this on first reading because it was so interesting to see Pinter being, as it were, Pinteresque on a *real* issue he obviously felt strongly about, brilliantly satirizing the politician's habit of converting ugly reality to pure rhetoric—an almost perfect description of what he is doing in *The Homecoming*. Listen to this same politician's language now in the mouths of Max and Lenny:

> *Sam*. . . . You know what he said to me? He told me I was the best chauffeur he'd ever had. The best one.
> *Max*. From what point of view?
> *Sam*. Eh?
> *Max*. From what point of view?
> *Lenny*. From the point of view of his driving, Dad, and his general sense of courtesy, I should say.

Or this passage taken from the family discussion of how Ruth is to be treated in her "various" roles:

> *Max*. Lenny, do you mind if I make a little comment? It's not meant to be critical. But I think you're concentrating too much on the economic considerations. There are other considerations. There are human considerations. You understand what I mean? There are the human considerations. Don't forget them.

Or take the peripety itself, in which the play arrives at its greatest gulf between manner and matter, a small masterpiece of collective one-upmanship:

> *Teddy*. Ruth . . . the family have invited you to stay for a little while longer. As a . . . a kind of guest. If you like the idea I don't mind. We can manage very easily at home . . . until you come back.
> *Ruth*. How very nice of them.
> *Pause*.

Max. It's an offer from our heart.
Ruth. It's very sweet of you.
Max. Listen . . . it would be our pleasure.

Altogether, it is an irony that disappears at times into pure comedy, reminding one of that old cartoon about the cannibal sporting the bowler and umbrella of the English gentleman he is about to eat.

Perhaps the most spectacular example of Pinter brutality to date is the scene in which Lenny recites his deeds to Ruth, his brother's wife (whom he has known less than five minutes):

> Well, this lady was very insistent and started taking liberties with me down under this arch, liberties which by any criterion I couldn't be expected to tolerate, the facts being what they were, so I clumped her one. It was on my mind at the time to do away with her, you know, to kill her, and the fact is, that as killings go, it would have been a simple matter, nothing to it. Her chauffeur, who had located me for her, he'd popped round the corner to have a drink, which just left this lady and myself, you see, alone, standing underneath this arch, watching all the steamers steaming up, no one about, all quiet on the Western Front, and there she was up against this wall —well, just sliding down the wall, following the blow I'd given her. Well, to sum up, everything was in my favour, for a killing. Don't worry about the chauffeur. The chauffeur would never have spoken. He was an old friend of the family. But . . . in the end I thought . . . Aaah, why go to all the bother . . . you know, getting rid of the corpse and all that, getting yourself into a state of tension. So I just gave her another belt in the nose and a couple of turns of the boot and sort of left it at that.

Now there is a serious question here as to whether Lenny really did this at all, much less with such terrifying indifference; but that is beside the point, just as it is beside the point to inquire whether the family is capable of having sex with Ruth. The main thing is the conception and framing of the possibility, the something *done* to the brutality that counts. The genial minimization of it, you might say. And Lenny accomplishes this by satirizing his act in the language his "betters" habitually use to sanitize themselves from dockside realities of just this sort. The effect, of course, is to make him superior to his brutality, to the class morality he is mimicking, and to his freshest opponent in what his soul-brother Mick, in *The Caretaker,* calls "the game." In a sense I think the actor will appreciate, life is *all* performance for Lenny, a veritable charade of politesse.

The question is, what does it mean to an audience? Is Pinter our Molière of the bullock-pen? Is he saying that insofar as language is supposed to correspond to deed and intent it is being "spilled," and the entire moral structure along with it? That the Family is taking out its spite against society by imitating it to its own "diseased" specifications (each character being an aspect of, first English, then "modern" decay), and that in order to avoid such corruption as theirs, as one critic has pointed out, we have got to pull together somehow, wake up to our encroaching dehumanization? Or, what seems a more commonly held view, that the play is simply descriptive of a condition we can do nothing about, given the persistence of the beast in the genes, but which it is the artist's instinct and duty to portray, in the belief that an aesthetic triumph over life is better than none at all? In short, what does the presence of such Irony, as the very *process* of the play, signify on our scene?

In the *Paris Review* article, Pinter was asked if he considered the world "an essentially violent place." Yes, it was violent all right, he said, but the violence was "really only an expression of the question of dominance and subservience," the repeated theme (he thought) of his plays. There is about Pinter's remarks on himself a very refreshing sense of the craftsman in his shop (or rather, *out* of it, and wanting to get back), and none of the displaced philosopher taking his chance to talk (art being mute). All questions, if possible, are converted to matters of technique—*"writing the bloody play!"* In his remark I think he has converted *our* world into his own artistic frame of reference very thoroughly: a question of dominance and subservience, a "common everyday thing." Reflecting it against the plays, the telling thing about it is its fixation on *the fact* of violence as a kind of source, or quarry to be mined, and its unconcern for the consequences of violence on the human scene. Does it not, in fact, bespeak a certain detachment that comes with accommodation to, or indifference toward, an "old" problem?

Now one might easily invoke here Chekhov's famous comeback to the accusation of indifference—"We don't have to be *told* that stealing horses is bad." In other words, the objective, no-comment depiction of malevolence carries its own power of denial and opposition, its own unfurled sympathy with health. And it undoubtedly does—when the artist *wants* it to and sees to it that the ironies are leaned in that direction. But I have never been convinced that Chekhov wanted it to and that he was not absolutely fascinated by the blackest possibilities of the void out of which Shestov said he created. Moreover, questions of this sort occur: Do we not underestimate the attractiveness of evil? Is not one of the pleasures of art evil's power to arrest for our delight certain bold lines of force which goodness simply doesn't possess? To bring it up to date, could we not be arriving at a kind of art (of which Pinter is our most daring example) which is showing signs of restlessness with its content and is therefore shifting its focus from an attention to the content for its own sake (our Absurd "condition") to the interesting symmetries inherent in it?

I seem to be suggesting that Pinter is callously producing what Mr. Wimsatt calls "vile art," art which presents immoral acts irresponsibly, if not with approval and joy (as we are told our movies are doing these days). I am not really prepared to argue that question; but I feel obliged to put Pinter into the context he deserves most and that amounts to considering him as a craftsman rather than a thinker, a maker of theatre out of "accepted" materials. In short, I find the question of whether he sees the world as "essentially violent" about as interesting and relevant to his art as whether, let us say, John Constable sees the world as essentially peaceful. And I would enlarge this idea along the following line:

It would appear that Absurdist violence, like all forms of radical experience "used" and then "used up" by artists, may be passing into its twilight or "aesthetic" stage and that our reactions to it are changing in subtle and remarkable ways, impossible to assess. We know very little about this strange passage in the arts in which moral actions figure powerfully as the content, but we are learning something about how greatly it influences the course of the graphic arts; and there seems no reason to exempt the drama from the implications of Wölfflin's well-known idea that paintings owe more to other paintings than they owe to nature; nor from E. H. Gombrich's more recent expansion of that general idea that it is "the power of expectation rather than the power of conceptual knowledge that molds what we see in life no less than in art." We see reality, in other words, in terms of our formulations of it.

It is not appropriate to develop this far-ranging idea in very great detail here, but one of the ways in which the power of expectation would seem to operate on the dramatic artist is in adjusting his field of vision between "what has been done," to put it simply, and "what is left to do," or, if you prefer, between the images of other artists (in and out of his medium) and the suggestions they carry for further expansion. Since violence is the natural content of all "serious" drama, it seems reasonable to assume that violence (to personify it) goes a progress through the available possibilities in a constant struggle to recapture its power of fascination; one of the ways it appears to do this, as I trust the history of drama will show, is to take daring permissions with its inherited conceptions of itself, to become by turns more particular, more inward, more subtle, more "free," more "immoral," more "real," more indifferent, more sophisticated, more paradoxical (a standard device for eluding discovery); to parody itself, to offer as much sensation as the traffic will bear, and so on, until it is finally performing with only a side glance at Nature herself, the reality observed being mainly the already formulated realities of the tradition to which it belongs. Fidelity to experience, moral qualm, truth, these are indeed perpetuated, but in the terms of the medium. Something of this sort seems to have been happening in the later Greek plays (*Orestes* comes to mind) and again in those chain-reactive monstrosities of lust and cruelty of the Jacobeans—the sort of plays, in other words, which our theatre is rapidly discovering as "surprisingly playable" and which critics are busy writing down as remarkable prefigurations of the existential view of life, or—if not that—as clear proofs of the author's disillusion with his age.

To what extent all this is reflective of external changes in moral patterns and tolerances it is probably not possible to say; certainly the interplay is greater than I am suggesting in this one-sided presentation and I am stating the whole case badly in forcing a separation of the insoluble marriage of Morals and Aesthetics. But it does seem to me that the incidence of irony on our scene (and I have discussed only one particular, if not rare, variety)—which has led Northrop Frye and others to conclude that irony is the characteristic fictional mode of our century—might be reckoned in our criticism as a somewhat less depressing thing than our loss of spiritual security. Does it not open also the possibility of irony's appeal as a form of more or less pure patterning, of the manipulation of "experience" into certain kinds of symmetries (the predictable operation of dissonance) which the mind finds innately interesting because (1) it appreciates symmetry of any kind, irrespective of its bearing on human ideals, and (2) at certain times in the flux of art traditions it craves the release of the ironic variation, the art, as Frye says, which has "no object but its subject" (or, as Empson says, the art which enables the artist to say "a plague on both your houses"). Thus, we might theorize that irony has two aspects: it is, in the moral sense, a defense against the failure of any single option to convince, the loss of a clear stake in an ideological inheritance; and, in the aesthetic sense, it is a defense against the exhaustion of a set of inherited images. No doubt there is an intricate relationship between the two (if *two* there are); the point I wish to make here is that in such movements there are such things as artists who are less interested in revealing us than in amazing us.

Getting back to Poe for a moment, I am reminded of a recent essay in *Kenyon Review* by Terence Martin who makes a case for Poe's "play habit," the "desire to astonish by boundless exaggeration or confusion of proportions." He is "our one author," says Mr. Martin, "who makes an absolute commitment to the imagination —who releases the imagination into a realm of its own where, with nothing to play *with,* it must play *at* our destruction. He shows us insistently that the imagination at his kind of play is not only anti-social but anti-human. To do justice to his contemporaries, perhaps we should say that what Poe undertook was not to be looked at without blinking."

That is more or less how I feel about Harold Pinter. In fact, with just a little transposing, we could probably derive most of the old Gothic essentials from our play: the nightmare setting, the double vision of the real and the super-real, the lurking fatality and inexplicable tyranny, the mysterious inspecificity and yet *utter* relevance of everything. Even—allowing for an unfortunate degeneration in our heroine—the central Gothic theme of the pale and lovely maiden *dominated* by the inscrutable sadist of the "nameless vice." This is not intended as a dismissal of either Pinter or Gothicism. If anything, it is a plug for art which produces reactions other than the shock of recognition, art in which the very limitedness of the artist to relatively outré kinds of experience and his ability to arouse the precise *sense* of that experience are the things to be praised. To me, Pinter falls brilliantly into this category and it is with considerable respect for him that I subscribe to his own evaluation of himself as "overblown tremendously" by people who "tend to make too much of a meal." This is not at all to deny the good chance that he may come out in the end as the Poe or Huysmans of the Absurdist theatre—a better fate, perhaps, than the one in store for some of our sterner moralists.

Mixing Memory and Desire: Pinter's Vision in *Landscape, Silence,* and *Old Times*

by Arthur Ganz

As the inhabitants of Eliot's waste land world fear the cruel April whose rains threaten the sheltering spiritual winter in which they live, so the focal characters of Harold Pinter's plays often find their insulated worlds menaced by the intrusion of some vital, elemental power. Despite the gulf of temperament that separates these two writers, both are concerned with the fate of those who have retreated from the claims of existence into an icy, protective sterility. But whereas the characters of *The Waste Land* confront the possibility of spiritual rebirth, those of Pinter's world must come to terms with a reawakening as sinister as it is vital. In *The Birthday Party,* Goldberg and McCann do indeed bring Stanley out of the apathy and infantilism into which he has retreated, but their doing so seems to involve for Stanley at least as much spiritual destruction as illumination. When the crude vitality of Mick draws Davies of *The Caretaker* away from the remote and impassive Aston, it leads the desperate tramp to betray his benefactor and destroy his only hope of safety. Although Ruth in *The Homecoming* escapes from what is to her the aridity of her life as a conventional mother and academic wife, she must accept the degradation of her role as prostitute to satisfy her thirst for the passionate vitality she finds with her adoptive family.

From the first Pinter has dealt with the conflict between two significant impulses of the inner self. One is toward a life of power, energy, and sexual gratification; but because this impulse is often associated with coarseness, perversion, or crude self-aggrandizement, it evokes a contrary impulse toward retreat, restraint, withdrawal, remoteness from life. The desire to shelter in a room, so often noted in Pinter's work, is a way of expressing in dramatic terms the desire to retreat from those impulses of the self that are both dangerous and alluring. The new life that burgeons in the psychic waste land may be a vital growth, but it is not a spiritual one.

Though the blatant power with which these ambiguous impulses surge through *The Homecoming* is much muted when Pinter returns to the theatre with the brief, contemplative, actionless *Landscape,* it is nonetheless present. Turning from the grand scope, the intense confrontations, the startling actions of *The Homecoming* to a drama of meditation, a theatre without movement, Pinter still remains committed to the exploration of the great antitheses that are the twin anchors of his work. Indeed, however different *Landscape* is from the major play that preceded it (and it is likely that Pinter intended it to be as different as possible) the opposition of force and delicacy, of passion and control, embodied in both *Landscape* and its companion piece, *Silence,* links them indissolubly to *The Homecoming* and to the general body of Pinter's work. *Silence* and *The Homecoming,* in fact, are in one aspect opposites: whereas the sexually active and powerful Ruth decisively chooses the passional life of her husband's family over the arid conventionalities of her life in America, Ellen, the heroine of *Silence,* fails to make a choice between the two suitors, who represent similar, though not identical, antitheses.

Landscape, however, poses a special problem, for here choice is both made and denied, while the manner of its frustration remains strangely elusive. In part it does so because of the special nature of the play itself, which consists entirely of two interlocked monologues: one, a rambling and apparently inconsequential account of the events of the day by the husband, Duff, addressed to his wife, Beth; the other, Beth's inner meditation on an experience of love long ago; both are delivered while the characters sit immobile and largely unrelated in the kitchen of a country house where they were once servants and are now owners or resident caretakers. Especially in performance the tangle of memory and event is difficult to unravel, and though the emotional distance between husband and wife is movingly apparent, the full significance of Duff's narrative and Beth's dreamlike recollections is hardly to be seen.[1] Even a close

[1] An attempt to solve this problem was made in the production at Lincoln Center in New York where the play was performed twice at each presentation.

reading of the text does not answer all the questions raised by Beth's memories, but it does bring Duff more clearly into focus.

Distanced from his wife by his inability to communicate his feeling for her—"I meant to tell you" is a phrase he repeats throughout the play—he is also separated from her by a difference in temperament. He is rougher, coarser, more physical than Beth, as suggested by the story he tells, which begins with images of excrement: "Mind you, there was a lot of shit all over the place, all along the paths, by the pond. Dogshit, duckshit . . . all kinds of shit . . . all over the paths." The story continues as he tells how "some nut" questioned the quality of the beer in a pub and how Duff crushed his pathetic and insecure opponent with claims to superior knowledge. The talk of beer barrels produces images of physical violence: "Spile the bung. Hammer the spile through the centre of the bung. That lets the air through the bung, down the bunghole [. . .]" [2] Since *bung* is both the hole in the beer barrel and the anus, these images have a strong sexual overtone, which culminates in his anger at Beth, when, in a moment of grief, she sounds the dinner gong in the empty house: "What the bloody hell are you doing banging that bloody gong? (*Pause.*) It's bullshit. [. . .] There's not a soul in the house. Except me. There's nothing for lunch. There's nothing cooked. No stew. No pie. No greens. No joint. Fuck all." The lack of food here suggests the lack of sexual life. In Duff's final speech images of animal gratification ("I would have had you in front of the dog"), longing ("I thought you would come into my arms and kiss me"), and sexual violence ("bang you against it swinging, gonging, waking the place up, calling them all for dinner, lunch is up, bring out the bacon") all merge in a richly symbolic characterization.

Duff embodies not only a crude physicality but a lack of sensibility as well. He says that he has thought of inviting people from the village into their solitary house for a drink, but then he adds, "I decided against it. It's not necessary." When he tells his wife that he briefly betrayed her, the same rigidity and authoritarianism recur. "The girl herself I considered unimportant. I didn't think it necessary to go into details. I decided against it." These qualities inevitably make his fragmentary attempts to communicate with his wife ineffectual. For Beth, at once more sensitive and less vital, has

[2] Since Pinter often uses three dots as punctuation, brackets have here been placed around dots indicating an editorial deletion.

retreated like other Pinter characters into the shelter of a room (she apparently does not go out of the house), and more importantly, she has also retreated into a world of memory. Throughout the play she remains lost in her recollections of a moment of emotional fulfillment on a beach with her lover, whom she remembers for his quiet gentleness. Her speech at the end of the play, which through rhythm, alliteration, and assonance Pinter elevates to the level of verse, is the climax of this vision.

He lay above me and looked down at me. He supported my shoulder.
Pause
My hand on his rib
Pause
So sweetly the sand over me. Tiny the sand on my skin.
Pause
So silent the sky in my eyes. Gently the sound of the tide.
Pause
Oh my true love I said.

The unity of man and woman evoked by the hinted reference to Adam's rib stands in sharp contrast to the actual separation of Duff and Beth.

Although this alienation is clearly at the center of the play, there remains an ambiguity in the action. A reader's first supposition is that the lover on the beach was Mr. Sykes, the employer of Beth and Duff who has died or gone away and apparently given them his house. "A gloomy bugger," as Duff calls him, he may have been peculiarly cruel to Beth. "Mr Sykes gave a little dinner party that Friday," Duff says. "He complimented you on your cooking and the service. (*Pause*) Two women. That was all. Never seen them before. Probably his mother and sister." There is little point in bringing into the play the recollection of the party and Beth's exhaustion ("You were asleep as soon as you hit the pillow. Your body . . . just fell back") unless the women were hired and paraded before Beth as an act of hostility. If the story concealed in Beth's reminiscences concerns a moody gentleman-lover, who seduces her, humiliates her, and leaves her hopelessly calling him by sounding the dinner gong in an empty house, it is very like a high Victorian melodrama. (Our memory of the brutal Bill Sykes reinforces the association.) One almost wonders if Mrs. Rochester, or at least Mrs. Sykes, is to be found chained in the attic. A very different reading of the play, however, comes from the author himself. Martin Esslin quotes a letter, made public accidentally and without Pinter's approval, to the director of the first German production of *Landscape,* in which Pinter says that "the man on the beach is Duff." But he goes on to say of Beth, "I think there are elements of Mr Sykes in her memory of this Duff," and adds that although Duff is jealous of Mr. Sykes, "I do not believe Mr Sykes and Beth were ever lovers. I formed these conclusions after I had written the plays and after learning about them [*Silence* is also referred to] through rehearsals." The letter, despite the definite statement that Duff is the man on the beach, implies that an opposing view might also be viable. Esslin, suggesting that "the point is, of course, that we will never be quite certain what the truth might be," concludes only that "the landscape of memory . . . is . . . shrouded in the mists of eternal uncertainty." [3]

But the richly suggestive complexity of the text demands that we do more than hedge our bets and admit that the past is unsure. Pinter's suggestion that in her memory Beth may be mingling the characters of Duff and Mr. Sykes offers us a clue to what he has wrought through his art without necessarily conceptualizing it fully. If *Landscape* is operating on two levels simultaneously, then Duff and Mr. Sykes are separate psychological persons on the realistic level, but on the symbolic one they are the familiar extremes of the human temperament. Beth longs for the gentleness and quiescence of Mr. Sykes, but these qualities are not to be separated from Duff's coarseness and physical demands. When Mr. Sykes flaunts other women before her, he betrays her, in effect, by becoming Duff. Beth longs to have a child by her lover on the beach, but to do so she must give herself to the active physicality of Duff (the lover on the beach is only remembered as asleep). Significantly, her meditation as she cleans the dishes the morning after the dinner party centers on her longing: "I saw children in the valley. They were running through the grass. They ran up the hill. (*Long silence.*)" (The importance of the lines is marked by that stage direction, the only such in the play.) Then, after an interruption by Duff, Beth resumes:

> I remembered always, in drawing, the basic principles of shadow and light. Objects intercepting the light cast shadows. Shadow is depriva-

[3] *The Peopled Wound: The Work of Harold Pinter* (New York: Doubleday & Company, Inc., 1970), p. 187.

> tion of light. The shape of the shadow is determined by that of the object. But not always. Not always directly. Sometimes the cause of the shadow cannot be found.

The delicate and the brutal are inextricably linked. "The cause," the reason that the shadow of the latter obliterates the light of the former is indeed hardly to be "found." And the balanced acceptance of these polarities, that might make life viable, is never achieved in Pinter's work.

Nor does *Landscape's* companion piece, *Silence,* though it is clearly a reworking of the same material, illuminate entirely the process by which fulfillment is denied and life dribbles away in solitude and frustration. Once again a woman is set between two men of contrasting temperament, though here there is no elusive figure apprehended, as Mr. Sykes is, only through memory. In *Silence* both men are solidly present on stage and both at moments actually speak with the woman, whereas in *Landscape* no actual conversation ever takes place. But *Landscape* was clearly set in the kitchen of a country house; in *Silence,* as if to offset its greater degree of dramatic contact among the characters, there is no delimiting of space or time. The setting is presented simply as "Three areas. A chair in each area," and, though the stage directions designate Ellen as "a girl in her twenties," Rumsey as "a man of forty," and Bates as "a man in his middle thirties," the play moves freely through their lives from the time Ellen is a child and the other two are young men to the point when all three are old. The ages designated by the stage directions and embodied in the actors are only those at which the decisive choices in their relationships are made.

As the play begins, they are at these designated ages, and each in a brief monologue, simple in diction but carefully patterned to lift it above the level of realistic conversation, suggests his situation and character. Although Rumsey has none of the moodiness and possible cruelty of Mr. Sykes, he shares with that figure, or at any rate with the man on the beach as Beth remembers him, a mildness and gentleness of manner that makes them both embodiments of quiescence, passivity, and grace. His relationship with Ellen is one of calm, thoughtful intimacy and, like that of Beth and the man on the beach, is associated with images of nature:

> On good evenings we walk through the hills to the top of the hill past the dogs the cloud racing just before dark or as dark is falling when the moon
>
> When it's chilly I stop her and slip her raincoat over her shoulders or rainy slip arms into the arms, she twisting her arms. And talk to her and tell her everything.

Bates, on the other hand, is rough, passionate, and demanding. He is, moreover, associated with the violence and crowding of the urban scene:

> Caught a bus to town. Crowds. Lights round the market, rain and stinking. Showed her the bumping lights. Took her down around the dumps. Black roads and girders. She clutching me. This way the way I bring you. Pubs throw the doors smack into the night. Cars barking and the lights. She with me, clutching

Between these two alternatives—the gentle pastoral quiescence and the crude urban vitality—the heroine is poised, attracted almost equally to both:

> There are two. I turn to them and speak. I look them in their eyes. I kiss them there and say, I look away to smile, and touch them as I turn.

Abruptly Pinter inserts the stage direction *Silence,* designating here and for the most part throughout the play the transition from one section to another. When the characters speak again, the audience recognizes that all are old. Rumsey has drifted off into a contented remoteness: "My heart never bangs. I read in the evenings. There is no-one to tell me what is expected or not expected of me. There is nothing required of me." Bates, also alone, rages passionately "without any true rest, having no solace, no constant solace, not even any damn inconstant solace," and denounces the young men about him with "their tittering bitches, and their music, and their love." But Ellen, the central figure, is the most severely traumatized of all. Remote even from her memories, she has entered into a state of mental separation in which the reality of her own thoughts becomes doubtful. "But I couldn't remember anything I'd actually thought, for some time," she says: "It isn't something that anyone could ever tell me, could ever reassure me about, nobody could tell, from looking at me, what was happening."

In the remaining part of the play Pinter gives us through interwoven fragments of thought and conversation some sense of how these lives have drifted off into solitude and emotional paralysis. As small pieces of experience are juxtaposed, we are led to recognize that both of the men embody qualities which have so equally attracted and repelled Ellen that she has finally remained motionless between them. Bates, for example, makes intense, but rough and inarticulate, sexual demands on Ellen: "Come with me tonight. [. . .] For a walk." Repelled and discontented, Ellen at first resists Bates' invitation to go to his cousin's place in town. But earlier in the play Bates had already told us, "Brought her into this place, my cousin runs it. Undressed her, placed my hand." And yet, for all his crudity, Bates is capable of kindness and empathy. He remembers taking Ellen for a walk when she was a child and finding her frightened by "something in a tree, a shape, a shadow." He had consoled her with kindly sympathy: "Maybe it's a bird, I said, a big bird, resting."

As a lover Rumsey is quite unlike Bates. Ellen remembers a visit to Rumsey's house, on which he approached her with gentleness and charm:

> He sat me on his knee, by the window, and asked if he could kiss my right cheek. I nodded he could. He did. Then he asked, if, having kissed my right, he could do the same with my left. I said yes. He did.

Yet when Ellen comes to him and asks for a more committed relationship, his answer is a frigid, regressive "Find a young man." Though she protests that she doesn't care for them, he can only reply, "You're stupid. [. . .] (*Pause*) Find one." Thus rejected, Ellen, like Beth of *Landscape,* has drifted off into a largely solitary existence in a world of memory. Here the surrounding people are, to her, insubstantial and even her memories uncertain. A woman companion asks Ellen "for the hundredth time" if she has ever been married. "This time I told her I had," Ellen recalls. "Yes, I told her I had. Certainly. I can remember the wedding." But we are forewarned against even this doubtful recollection when, just before these words, Ellen says, "And then often it is only half things I remember, half things, beginnings of things." Even though Ellen, between the passion of Bates and the quiescence of Rumsey, has found no life, even though the wedding was only one of those "half things, beginnings of things," it remains, as the play turns into jumbled fragments of earlier dialogue and disintegrates into the silence of its title, suspended in memory, for Ellen's last sad words are the repetition of "Certainly. I can remember the wedding."

As these words suggest, Ellen's life is dominated by the memory of a past which, however elusive and uncertain, has had a sinister power in shaping the present. This great Ibsenite theme—of the weight of the past—begins to appear significantly in Pinter's work with *The Homecoming,* as Ruth broods over her earlier life in England and feels it drawing her back. (Figures from the past enter into *The Room* and *The Birthday Party,* but in these plays the past *per se* is not emphasized thematically.) In the dramatic sketches, *Landscape* and *Silence,* Pinter explores the theme, and finally in *Old Times* he lets it flower out as a central motif of a longer play.[4] But whereas in Ibsen the past is a chartered countryside through which one makes a sure and progressive journey to some point of illumination, in Pinter the past is a misty wasteland into which one makes sporadic forays, returning with fragments of insight and information which contradict and confuse as much as they enlighten. Nor is it surprising that the journey through the past should yield such dubious matter. Though Pinter, now in his forties, is old enough to sense the past as an area sufficiently large and obscure to be worth exploring (it is there, after all, that crucial choices were made), he is still searching for the resolution to that opposition, of quiescence and vitality, which has haunted his work from its beginning. The intruders in Pinter's plays have always tended to be impulses from the inner self; as his work has become more subtle and more clearly focussed on that inner life, the gangster from the void has been transformed into the living memory of the past. But given the fundamental antipathy of these impulses he is no more likely to find a resolution in the world of memory than in that of the sinister present.

Indeed, whether or not *Old Times* reflects a new concern with the past by Pinter, it reveals most strikingly the continuity of his work by its linkage with his earliest play. Though *Old Times* is clearly related to *Landscape* and *Silence* by its concern with memory,

[4] Pinter's screenplay for the film *The Go Between,* written during the period of these plays, is also concerned with the sinister and mysterious power of the past over the present.

its restraint (all three plays suggest a sort of dramatic chamber music) and its concentrated size, its basic dramatic situation recalls that of *The Room.* In both plays the central figure is a woman who lives with her husband in a remote and sheltered place, Rose in her room and Kate in a converted farmhouse by the sea—"permanently in such a silence," as Anna, the friend of her youth who returns after twenty years, describes it. Both husbands are, or appear to be, forcefully masculine persons who upon occasion leave the home, Bert to drive his van, Deeley to pursue his work as a filmmaker. Moreover, in each play the shelter is invaded by a figure from the woman's past—the blind Negro in *The Room,* Anna in *Old Times*—who demands that she assume a relationship with that part of her life, and in each case the husband fights fiercely and brutally to repel the threatened intrusion. Beyond these similarities, the plays are, as one would expect of works written at such different stages of Pinter's career, very different in style and content; the invading figure in *The Room,* for example, seems essentially benign, whereas Anna is a sinister creation. But such inevitable differences reflect the development of Pinter's art rather than any fundamental alteration of his vision.

In *Old Times* the state of quiescence is associated with Kate, as she appears through most of the play. Not only has Anna described Kate's present condition of life as "a silence," but she says that Kate had always been a dreamer who would literally lose track of what day it was. Deeley too says that his wife "hasn't made many friends, although there's been every opportunity for her to do so." "She lacks curiosity," he adds accusingly. The main feature of Kate's life, in fact, seems to be long, solitary walks. "Sometimes I walk to the sea," she says abruptly. "There aren't many people. It's a long beach." And up until almost the end of the play Kate remains uncommunicative, remote, and enigmatic while Deeley and Anna battle fiercely in their attempts to possess her.

Even before Anna enters the dialogue, Deeley is aggressive and suspicious of her. When Kate, reminiscing about the past, mentions that Anna used to steal from her "Bits and pieces. Underwear," Deeley after a pause suddenly asks, "Is that what attracted you to her?" A moment later Deeley's suspicions come to the surface again as he tells his wife that he will be interested in her reactions to her old friend's visit. "I'll be watching you," he says to Kate. As Deeley and Kate speak, Anna has been standing apart—the past incarnate—visibly present on stage though not yet realistically recognized by the others, but almost as soon as she joins the conversation, Deeley attacks her with a characteristic Pinter weapon, words. When she uses the term *lest,* Deeley pounces upon it. "The word lest," he exclaims in mock astonishment. "Haven't heard it for a long time." Shortly after, when Anna speaks of Kate as having at a certain moment been unaware of her gaze, Deeley again seizes upon the term. "The word gaze. Don't hear it very often." Deeley here implies that Anna is affected and snobbish in her speech but suggests that his own is decisive and controlled. Pointing out that his work takes him all over the globe, he adds, "I use the word globe because the word world possesses emotional political sociological and psychological pretensions and resonances which I prefer as a matter of choice to do without, or shall I say to steer clear of, or if you like to reject." But though Deeley exalts his own speech and criticizes Anna's, he nevertheless asserts power by stealing her language. Anna, reminiscing about Kate, had described her as looking around and "flicking her hair." Shortly after, Deeley, talking about his first meetings with Kate, says that she "looked at me [. . .] flicking her hair back."

But this fencing with words, though revelatory, is only peripheral skirmishing. The battle is joined seriously when Anna's reminiscences lead her and Deeley to vie with each other in singing snatches of old popular songs. The conventional lyrics inevitably become claims and appeals to Kate:

> *Anna.* (*Singing.*) Oh but you're lovely, with your smile so warm . . .
> *Deeley.* (*Singing.*) I've got a woman crazy for me. She's funny that way.

When this melodious rivalry is inconclusive, Deeley abruptly launches his major attack. Like Lenny, of *The Homecoming,* he asserts his power and masculinity by telling stories in which he possesses these qualities and in which women appear as degraded or subservient creatures, for he is attempting not only to fight off Anna but to force Kate to accept the status of his possession. On a "bloody awful summer afternoon," Deeley tells us he "popped into a fleapit" (the phrases denigrate both the time and place at which he meets Kate) to see the film *Odd Man Out.* He remembered at the time that in that very neighborhood his father had bought him his first and only tricycle. The association at once trivializes Kate, reducing her to the level of a toy, and exalts her to the status of a sacred possession to be protected with childish savagery. Indeed, Deeley's next words suggest the fierceness of his attack even as they reveal some of the sources of his doubts: "and there were two usherettes standing in the foyer and one of them was stroking her breasts and the other one was saying 'dirty bitch' and the one stroking her breasts was saying 'mmnnn' with a very sensual relish and smiling at her fellow usherette. [. . .]" Though the usherettes, surrogates for Kate and Anna, are presented in the lesbian relationship that Deeley fears, the atmosphere is squalid and one is hostile to the other—as if by magical transference Deeley could make Kate angry with Anna. (There is even a touch of homosexual revenge in Deeley's passionate admiration for the performance of Robert Newton: "And I would commit murder for him, even now.") But Deeley's major attack comes when he describes his meeting with Kate, who was sitting "at the dead centre of the auditorium." "I was off centre and have remained so," Deeley admits in a parenthetic moment of bitter symbolism (in this sense he is the odd man out). He then goes on to explain how, as they were walking out after the film, his remark about Robert Newton's performance initiated a conversation with Kate:

> [. . .] and I thought Jesus this is it, I've made a catch, this is a trueblue pickup, and when we had sat down in the cafe with tea she looked into her cup and then up at me and told me she thought Robert Newton was remarkable. So it was Robert Newton who brought us together and it is only Robert Newton who can tear us apart.

Though Deeley assumes an air of masculine contempt for the "trueblue pickup" and introduces a grotesque version of the cliché as to what "brought us together," he ends with a warning to Anna (parodying yet invoking the marriage service) against attempting to "tear us apart." His power and possession, he warns, are not to be denied.

But Anna's claims are equally intense, and Deeley's weapons are available to her also. She too can tell stories and makes clear that the point is not their truth but their power. "There are things I remember," she warns Deeley, "which may never have happened but as I recall them so they take place." Then she launches into a story of the time when she and Kate lived together. Arriving home one night, she found "this man crying in our room" while Kate sat silently on the bed. The man, she says, continued sobbing as Anna undressed, turned out the light, and got into bed. Then after a time he stopped and came over to her, but, she says, "I would have absolutely nothing to do with him, nothing." And a moment later she repeats the phrase, only slightly varied, "I would have nothing to do with him, absolutely nothing." The man left, but Anna says that later in the night she woke and saw him on Kate's bed: "He was lying across her lap on her bed."

At least two purposes are served by the story. It allows Anna to attack Deeley's claims of masculine power (we accept the man as Deeley even before he so identifies himself in performing these acts at the end of the play) by portraying him as abjectly humiliated by some personal or sexual failure. Moreover, the story allows Pinter to identify Anna as an aspect of Kate—her passional self, from which she has retreated in her heterosexual, domestic relationship with Deeley. No actual roommate—however possessed of *sang froid*—is likely to retire quietly to bed under the circumstances Anna describes. When Anna will have "absolutely nothing to do with" the man who approaches her bed, she embodies Kate's refusal to grant Deeley the passionate arousal he desires from her. His tears are of no avail, for Kate will accept him only in a submissive, childlike position, "lying across her lap on her bed."

In Pinter's work symbolic relationships, such as the one suggested here, must always be assessed with care and tact. Anna is both a real character and a symbolic presence; indeed, she can be both at the same time. When Deeley stands by at the end of Act I and allows his wife to be possessed spiritually by Anna (as the two women drift off into the life of the past), the scene, though more subtle theatrically, is only a little less startling in concept than that in *The Homecoming* when Teddy stands by and allows his wife to be possessed physically by his brothers. In both cases the real external act carries a weight of suggestion that makes it symbolic of an internal psychological movement.

But the moment in Act I at which Anna and Kate are most strikingly identified comes as Anna describes the time when, at Kate's urging, they went to an obscure district and "almost alone, saw a wonderful film called Odd Man Out." Anna's claim to have been present at the time Deeley and Kate met is not merely a challenge to the truth of Deeley's story by a lesbian rival but an assertion that, as an aspect of Kate's inner self, she has always been with them, just as she is actually, though not ostensibly, present onstage as the play begins. Indeed, the mingling of the two women's identities becomes especially apparent near the end of Act II when Deeley, again telling a story, explains to Kate that he had met Anna twenty years ago and while taking her to a party had bought her a cup of coffee. "She thought she was you," he tells his wife, "said little, so little. Maybe she was you. Maybe it was you, having coffee with me, saying little, so little."

Originally, Deeley had intended the story told in Act II as another attack on Anna, designed to reduce her to something subservient to male sexual power. When he describes her as having been a habituée of a pub called The Wayfarer's Tavern, "the darling of the saloon bar," and as having at a party allowed him to spend the evening gazing up her skirt ("you didn't object, you found my gaze perfectly acceptable"), he is attempting to force a passive feminine role upon her and through her upon Kate who, he implies, was also at the party. In degrading language Deeley describes Kate and Anna as having "chatted and chuckled," sitting "squealing and hissing" while he gazed at their thighs and stockings.

But Anna, who at first denies her acquaintance with Deeley and her presence at the party, later turns the material of the story to her advantage. Picking up a motif that Pinter had posited in the first act, she tells Deeley that she was wearing Kate's underwear at the time Deeley looked up her skirt and that Kate, though she blushed when told, insisted thereafter that Anna sometimes borrow her underwear and then, as the two women sat in the dark, tell her "anything of interest" that occurred while she was wearing it.[5] By so adroitly turning the story in a new direction Anna warns Deeley that there is concealed in Kate a powerful sexual presence and hints that she is its embodiment.

[5] Significantly, Kate and Deeley, who share the exile from life in the house by the ocean—Deeley leaves it only to photograph other people—have a tendency toward vicarious sexual experience; Deeley only looks up Anna's skirt, Kate is a kind of voyeuse at one remove. When Deeley invites Anna to supervise while he dries and powders Kate, he is both teasing Anna by in effect offering his wife to her and at the same time inviting her to join them in a voyeuristic activity that leads to stimulation but not to erotic action. Indeed, Deeley seems to feel that the experience will make Anna and Kate quiescent, will "kill two birds with one stone," as he says.

However, one must be careful in Pinter not to oversimplify. Anna is not to be reduced to a simple allegorical element. Her sinister grace and composure carry a range of suggestions, all of which are relevant to her meaning in the play. Not only does she live "on a volcanic island" with its suggestions of passion, but she has a villa high on a cliff and sails on a yacht. These associations of *la dolce vita* are characterized by Deeley, whose speech shows traces of lower-class diction, as "a kind of elegance we know nothing about, a slim-bellied Côte d'Azur thing we know absolutely nothing about, a lobster and lobster sauce ideology we know fuck all about, the longest legs in the world, the most phenomenally soft voices." Anna, then, is at once an independent character, an aspect of Kate's inner self, and an embodiment of a whole tendency toward luxurious corruption and sophistication that Deeley fears.

But whereas Deeley, with his crude masculinity, is ultimately helpless, Kate reveals herself at the end of the play as the true possessor of power. Though she has retreated from the urgency and corruption of life to the countryside near the sea where "everything is softer" and lacks definition (indeed, she longs for a further retreat to "somewhere where you can look through the flap of a tent and see sand," a place reminiscent of the sterile desert Ruth has known in *The Homecoming*), nevertheless, when sufficiently threatened, she can assert herself. As the desired sexual object she, like Ruth, has power over those who desire her, though Ruth's power lies in the promise of sexuality, Kate's in the denial. Kate has, in fact, the power to kill, that is to refuse herself to those who desire her and thus to deny the life they would have through possession of her.

When the struggle between Deeley and Anna reaches its climax, Kate suddenly rouses herself and turns to Anna, saying, "I remember you dead." The line is in part her revenge on Anna, who had spoken of Kate as if she were dead in Act I, but it is essentially a reminder that Kate has the power to deny Anna's existence, to withdraw from the passional life she embodies. Kate continues:

> I remember you lying dead. You didn't know I was watching you. I leaned over you. Your face was dirty. You lay dead, your face scrawled with dirt, all kinds of earnest inscriptions, but unblotted, so that they had run, all over your face, down to your throat. [. . .] When you woke my eyes were above you, staring down at you. You tried to do my little trick, one of my tricks you had borrowed, my little slow smile

> [. . .] but it didn't work, the grin only split the dirt at sides of your mouth and stuck. You stuck in your grin. [. . .] Your bones were breaking through your face. But all was serene. There was no suffering. It had all happened elsewhere.

Like Deeley and Anna, Kate is telling a story, one that gives her power and defines her position. She has killed her vital but corrupt self and rejected its passionate appeals (the "unblotted" "earnest inscriptions"). Despite Anna's attempt to maintain her identity with Kate through the "little trick" that Anna emulates, Kate affirms her psychic withdrawal from that self and its death, which "happened elsewhere." But Kate also uses a "little trick" to suggest equally her remoteness from Deeley's conventional heterosexual demands. By attempting to plaster his face with dirt she affirms that he too is dead to her. Though she accepted Deeley's proposal of a wedding and a "change of environment," "neither mattered." These figures remain forever as we see them in the moment of illumination—literal and metaphorical—at the end of the play: Deeley, with his conventional masculine claims and attitudes, humiliated and in despair; Anna, the passional self, lying on her divan, dead and yet eternally latent within; Kate, maintaining her equilibrium between these intolerable alternatives by living (like Ellen) withdrawn in a psychic blur where nothing has shape or form.

Old Times, with its subtlety and understatement, lacks the immediate dramatic force of *The Birthday Party* or *The Homecoming* (though it is not less sinister, only less violent), but it has its own place in the body of Pinter's work, for it offers us its particular versions of the themes that Pinter has sounded before. Even the characters, however poised and remote—Anna is mysterious, symbolic; Kate is withdrawn to the point of psychosis; only Deeley, aggressive and desperate, seems immediately human—have a certain weight and force when we see them as legitimate descendants of those figures who stalked through Pinter's earlier plays. For Anna, with her associations of passion, luxury, and worldly power, is despite her sophistication and feminine grace an ally of Goldberg and Mick. Kate's condition of psychic withdrawal reminds us of Stanley, Teddy, and Aston, all of whom had preceded her into a similar state. Deeley, though he recalls Teddy and Duff in his desire to possess his wife and hold her apart from the world of greater passion, suggests even more strongly Davies confronting the two brothers: one remote and withdrawn, the other full of worldly energy and visions of luxury. (To some extent Lenny also confronts his two brothers, who similarly represent antitheses.) As Mick and Aston, as well as Teddy and Joey, are separate characters and yet brothers, opposing aspects of the inner self, so Anna and Kate remain genuinely differentiated dramatic figures and yet, we assume, as lesbian lovers, embodiments of those same impulses toward sensual freedom, power (as well as away from these qualities) that have always been the concern of Pinter's work.

As a Romantic artist, Pinter his known as much as any modern playwright the appeal of the liberated self. He has sensed, and embodied in the plays, that impulse toward the unlimited expansion of the ego, toward dominance, luxury, action, possession, sensual gratification. But as a late and disillusioned Romantic, Pinter has also known from the first that such an impulse was not to be trusted, that such qualities were as destructive as gratifying. Davies of *The Caretaker* is as near as Pinter has come to drawing a portrait of archetypal man; and though we pity Davies because he is, like all of us, weak, ignorant, lost on an endless journey, subject to age and death, nevertheless, we know that the endless self-aggrandizement of so vain and dangerous a creature cannot go unchecked. Yet so pressed are Pinter's characters by the demands of the self that the only way they can escape them is through total retreat into some state of withdrawal—some room—where they will be sheltered. Persons such as Stanley, Aston, Teddy, and Kate are not hiding from the I.R.A., or the trauma of a mental home, or a coarse family, or a lesbian past but from the demands of the inner self.

Pinter has often spoken of his admiration for Samuel Beckett, and his stylistic debt to the great symbolist playwright is easily enough perceived. Yet, though he shares Beckett's recognition of human vanity and fallibility, Pinter lacks the Irish writer's sense of the metaphysical on the one hand and his humane whimsy on the other. Of all the major modern playwrights, Pinter seems in certain essentials most closely allied to one comparatively distant in time and very different in style, Henrik Ibsen. Pinter shares with Ibsen a kind of grim humor, but more significantly, an essentially ambiguous view of the human condition. Both have given us figures possessed by a desire for self-aggrandizement, dominance, fulfillment, yet forever held back in a state of psychic paralysis.[6] If he were not still trailing some clouds of Faustian glory, the Master Builder might find a place in a Pinter play; Hilda Wangel, the embodiment of feminine power, would probably not object to making certain contractual arrangements with Lenny and his family in *The Homecoming*. For the creators of Solness and Davies, of Hilda and Ruth, are both attracted by the power of the vital inner self and repelled by its ruthlessness. That there should be so marked a similarity between the first great modern playwright and the writer who has most recently assumed a place in the line of descent from him suggests not only a coincidence in personality but the extent to which the modern drama is a body of Romantic art. And as the Romantic writer has characteristically turned to the past as a source of fulfillment, so Pinter, in *Landscape, Silence,* and *Old Times,* has sought there for the resolution to the contradictions with which he has been concerned. If his search has not brought us answers, it has brought us his plays, which are significant records of his quest.

[6] See R. F. Storch, "Harold Pinter's Happy Families" (reprinted in this volume), for a comparison between Pinter's dwarfs and Ibsen's.

Chronology of Important Dates

1930	Pinter is born in the East End of London, son of a hard-working but unsuccessful Jewish tailor.
1939	Is evacuated from London at the beginning of the war, at first to Cornwall, later nearer home.
1948	Receives London County Council grant to study at the Royal Academy of Dramatic Art but leaves after a short time. Refuses National Service (military duty) as a conscientious objector, though not on religious grounds.
1950	First published works, two poems, appear in *Poetry London.*
1951–1952	Tours Ireland playing Shakespeare in the acting company of Anew McMaster.
1953–1957	Acts with Donald Wolfit and in various provincial repertory theatres.
1956	Marries actress Vivien Merchant.
1957	Pinter's first play, *The Room,* written in four days, is produced by the Drama Department of Bristol University and then by the drama school of the Bristol Old Vic. This production attracts the attention of Harold Hobson, drama critic of the London *Sunday Times.*
1958	Pinter's son is born. *The Birthday Party,* produced in May at the Lyric Theatre, Hammersmith, is widely criticized, although defended by Harold Hobson and withdrawn after a week.
1959	May: *The Birthday Party* is performed more successfully by a semi-professional group. A revue containing two sketches by Pinter opens at the Lyric, Hammersmith, and *A Slight Ache* is broadcast by the B.B.C. Third Programme.

1960 *The Room* and *The Dumb Waiter* open in January at the Hampstead Theatre Club and are transferred in March to the Royal Court. *A Night Out* is broadcast by the B.B.C. in March and televised in April; Pinter and Vivien Merchant act in both productions. *The Birthday Party* is also televised in March. On April 27th *The Caretaker* opens at the Arts Theatre Club and transfers to a regular theatre in May. In July Pinter receives his first professional production in the United States, a staging of *The Birthday Party* at the Actors Workshop in San Francisco. In December *The Dwarfs* is broadcast by the B.B.C. Third Programme.

1961 *The Collection* is televised. October: *The Caretaker* opens in New York.

1962 *The Collection* is staged. *The Servant,* directed by Joseph Losey, with screenplay by Pinter, opens in London in November, and in December filming of *The Caretaker* begins.

1963 *The Lover* is televised and later staged with *The Dwarfs.*

1964 *The Birthday Party* is revived in London.

1965 June: *The Homecoming* opens in London.

1966 Pinter is made a Commander of the Order of the British Empire.

1967 January: *The Homecoming* is produced in New York and wins the Tony and New York Drama Critics' Circle awards. The film *Accident* is shown. Pinter directs Robert Shaw's play *The Man in the Glass Booth. The Birthday Party* is produced in New York.

1968 The Lord Chamberlain demands cuts in *Landscape,* which Pinter refuses. The Play is broadcast uncut on the B.B.C. Third Programme, radio not being under the Lord Chamberlain's authority. *The Birthday Party* is filmed. *The Tea Party* and *The Basement,* originally television plays, are staged in New York.

1969 *Landscape* and *Silence* are staged in London.

1970 *Landscape* and *Silence* are produced (at the small, experimental Forum Theatre of Lincoln Center) in New York.

1971 *The Birthday Party* (at the Forum) and *The Homecoming* are both revived in New York. *Old Times* is produced in London and New York.

Notes on the Editor and Contributors

ARTHUR GANZ, the editor of this volume, has published essays on Chekhov, Shaw, Wilde, Giraudoux, and other modern playwrights. He is an Associate Professor of English at The City College of The City University of New York.

JAMES T. BOULTON is Professor of English at the University of Nottingham. He is the author of *The Language of Politics in the Age of Wilkes and Burke* and has also published essays on D. H. Lawrence as well as a collection of letters by him, *Lawrence in Love: Letters to Louie Burrows.*

RUBY COHN is the author of *Samuel Beckett: The Comic Gamut*; *Currents in Contemporary Drama;* and numerous other books and articles. An editor of the journal *Modern Drama,* she has taught at the University of California at Santa Cruz and at the California Institute of the Arts. She is presently on the faculty of the University of California at Davis.

MARTIN ESSLIN, the head of Radio Drama for the British Broadcasting Corporation, is an influential critic of the modern drama. His books include *Brecht: A Choice of Evils, The Theatre of the Absurd,* and *The Peopled Wound: The Work of Harold Pinter.* He has also edited the Twentieth Century Views volume on Samuel Beckett.

JOHN LAHR, who writes drama criticism for *The Village Voice,* received the 1968–69 George Jean Nathan Award for Dramatic Criticism. Some of his work has been collected in *Up Against the Fourth Wall.* He is the author of a biography of his father, the late Bert Lahr, *Notes on a Cowardly Lion.*

VALERIE MINOGUE has taught French and Italian at University College, Cardiff, Wales, and is currently lecturer in French at London University. Mrs. Minogue has published poetry and essays on such writers as Alfred de Vigny and Alain Robbe-Grillet.

JOHN PESTA has held a Fulbright Fellowship at London University and taught at the University of Wisconsin—Parkside. He is the editor of the *Washington County Press,* a southern Indiana weekly.

Bert O. States, Associate Professor in the Department of Theatre Arts at Cornell, has also taught at Skidmore and The University of Pittsburgh. The author of *Irony and Drama: A Poetics,* he has in addition published articles in *The Hudson Review, The Yale Review,* and other journals.

R. F. Storch was born in Czechoslovakia, studied at Oxford, and has taught at the University of Ghana, Dartmouth, and Tufts. He has published articles on Wordsworth as well as on Neo-African culture and educational problems in West Africa.

John Russell Taylor writes on film for *The Times* of London. He is the author of *Cinema Eye, Cinema Ear*; *The Rise and Fall of the Well-Made Play*; and *Anger and After* as well as essays in various English magazines.

Selected Bibliography

Pinter's plays are published, in differing combinations, by Methuen & Co. Ltd. in England and by Grove Press in the United States. Several interviews with Pinter have been published, and most are listed in the bibliography of Martin Esslin's *The Peopled Wound.* Of Pinter's miscellaneous writings the following are of special interest:

Poems. Selected by Alan Clodd. London: Enitharmon Press, 1968.

Mac. London: Emanuel Wax for Pendragon Press, 1968. (A brief, lively memoir of Pinter's tour of Ireland in the Shakespearean company of Anew McMaster.)

"Between the Lines." (London) *Sunday Times,* 4 March 1962, p. 25. (A speech Pinter delivered at the Seventh National Students Drama Festival in Bristol.)

Five Screenplays. London: Methuen & Co. Ltd., 1971. (*The Servant, The Pumpkin Eater, The Quiller Memorandum, Accident, The Go-Between.*)

The amount of critical work that has appeared on an author who, as of this writing, has barely turned forty illustrates both the remarkable status of Pinter as a dramatist and the sometimes depressing professionalism of modern literary study. Listed below are two useful bibliographies, books in English, and a selected group of articles:

Bibliographies

Gordon, Lois G. "Pigeonholing Pinter: A Bibliography." *Theatre Documentation,* 1 (1968), 3–20.

Palmer, D. S. "Harold Pinter Checklist." *Twentieth Century Literature,* 16 (1970), 287–96.

Books in English

Burkman, Katherine H. *The Dramatic World of Harold Pinter: Its Basis in Ritual.* Columbus: Ohio State University Press, 1971.

Esslin, Martin. *The Peopled Wound: The Work of Harold Pinter.* New York: Doubleday & Company, Inc., Anchor Books, 1970. (Although it relies too heavily on mere summaries, this book is the best one so far available on Pinter.)

Hinchliffe, Arnold P. *Harold Pinter.* Twayne English Authors Series. New York: Twayne Publishers, Inc., 1967.

Hollis, James R. *Harold Pinter: The Poetics of Silence.* Carbondale: Southern Illinois University Press, 1970.

Lahr, John, ed. *A Casebook on Harold Pinter's* The Homecoming. New York: Grove Press, Inc., 1971.

Shorter Studies

Cohn, Ruby. "Latter Day Pinter." *Drama Survey,* 3 (1964), 367–77.

Dukore, Bernard. "The Theatre of Harold Pinter." *Tulane Drama Review,* 6 (1962), 43–54.

———. "A Woman's Place." *Quarterly Journal of Speech,* 52 (1966), 237–41.

Esslin, Martin. "Harold Pinter" in *The Theatre of the Absurd.* New York: Doubleday & Company, Inc., Anchor Books, 1961.

Gallagher, Kent G. "Harold Pinter's Dramaturgy." *Quarterly Journal of Speech,* 52 (1966), 242–48.

Ganz, Arthur. "A Clue to the Pinter Puzzle: The Triple Self in *The Homecoming.*" *Educational Theatre Journal,* 21 (1969), 180–87.

Kunkel, Francis L. "The Dystopia of Harold Pinter." *Renascence,* 21 (1968), 17–20.

Leech, Clifford. "Two Romantics: Arnold Wesker and Harold Pinter." *Contemporary Theatre,* 20 (1963), 11–31.

Mast, Gerald. "Pinter's *Homecoming.*" *Drama Survey,* 6 (1968), 266–77.

Morris, Kelly. "The Homecoming." *Tulane Drama Review,* 11 (1966), 185–91.

Nelson, Hugh. *"The Homecoming:* Kith and Kin" in *Modern British Dramatists: A Collection of Critical Essays.* Twentieth Century Views series. John Russell Brown, ed. Englewood Cliffs, N.J.: Prentice-Hall, Inc., 1968.

Schechner, Richard. "Puzzling Pinter." *Tulane Drama Review,* 11 (1966), 176–84.